Geography Around the World

by Margaret Parrish

illustrated by Tom Heggie

cover design by Jeff Van Kanegan
Photo credit: GlobeShots™

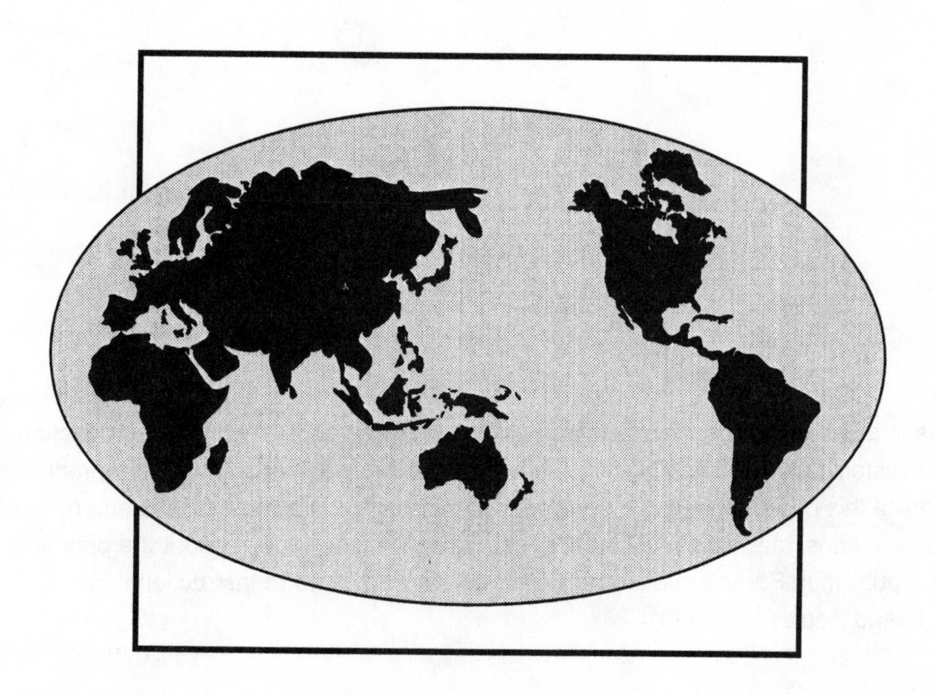

Publisher
Instructional Fair • TS Denison
Grand Rapids, Michigan 49544

ISBN: 1-56822-437-0
Geography Around the World

2400 Turner Avenue NW
Grand Rapids, Michigan 49544

Table of Contents

Introduction

One of the proven methods of gaining geographic knowledge is by studying the layout of our world—this is geography. One documented strategy for understanding geography is studying the five geographic themes. These provide a simple framework which will help the teacher to cover "all the bases" in teaching students the geography of the world.

This book is formatted around the regions of the world. Since there are various interpretations of what constitutes any of the world's regions, a regional delineation has been followed that has been recognized for the past two decades as the most comprehensive and accurate.

For the study of a world region, it is important to have a fundamental understanding of the region's location. Location tells us where in the world an area is found. Absolute location, such as latitude and longitude, is one method of answering "where." These coordinates give us an exact point on a globe or map for finding any place. If absolute placement is not practical, relative location provides another method for answering "where." Relative location is more generic and gives us a broader description of any place's location on earth by using descriptive words. With these two methods, students can identify and locate any area to be studied.

A second way to understand a region is to study its characteristics—physical and human. These answer the question "what" and give distinct meaning to any given place. Physical aspects of a place include atmospheric, biological, geological, and hydrological methods that produce landforms, water bodies, climate, soils, natural vegetation, and animal life. Human characteristics of a place include population features, languages, ideologies, economics, politics, architecture, and recreational activities. Studying these two attributes of place gives us a key to identifying and interpreting interrelations between people and their environments and among various groups of people.

The third theme of geography is human-environment interaction, which is the way people modify and adapt to their surroundings. Consequences of these modifications and adaptations impact us all in our globally interdependent world. Each place has its distinctive patterns of human-environment relationships. This theme answers some of the "how" and "why" questions of our world.

Movement is what allows humans to interact in our world. Communication and transportation systems enable people to link globally. Interaction changes as systems of movement change. With people, goods, and ideas being carried locally and worldwide, our knowledge goes with them. Movement begins to answer the question "how."

The fifth theme of geography is regions, which is the basic unit of geographical studies. Any area that exhibits unity in some way can be defined as a region. Regions provide a convenient method upon which to build our knowledge of our world. They define, examine, describe, explain, and analyze every aspect of the social sciences.

These five themes are so interrelated that it is difficult to teach one without the others. Students will use hands-on skills, map and globe study, and absolute and relative location to enhance their knowledge of geography. Following this format will ensure that all of the important material is covered.

Africa

Where Is Africa?

Themes of Geography: *Location, Place, Region*

Objectives

Students will
1. use globe, atlases, and maps to identify location of hemispheres
2. identify absolute location of natural features in Africa
3. examine map projections centered on Africa
4. describe relative location of African cities

Rationale

A globe is the best representation of the earth. As a scale model, a globe allows the earth to be viewed in proper proportions. The hemispheres (halves of the earth's sphere) can be identified directionally or as land or water.

Whenever a globe is flattened to make a map, some distortion (change) occurs. Every map has some distortion. Different maps can be designed by projecting a globe onto paper. Many map projections are computer designed. Each type of map projection has advantages and disadvantages. Many cartographers (map makers) feel the Robinson projection offers the best compromise in showing shapes and sizes of the earth's features on a map.

Skills Taught in This Unit

Globe and map reading
- Use of globe(s)
- Use of map projections
- Absolute location
- Latitude and longitude
- Relative location

Place characteristics
Region characteristics

Vocabulary

globe
plane
distortion
longitude
cylindrical
populous
interrupted
map
latitude
conic
relative location
cartographer
hemisphere
projection
absolute location
plane projections

Absolute Location in Africa

To study Africa's absolute location is to study a part of the world with many strategic geographical coordinates. This is the only continent situated in all four hemispheres. With the Gulf of Guinea at the intersection of the equator and prime meridian, it provides a perfect place to emphasize latitude and longitude.

Many world map projections have Africa centered on them. Cartographers continue to place this continent as a focal point of the map. Distortion created by various map projections often gives Africa an elongated appearance.

Materials: globe(s), atlases or other reference books, pencils, "Absolute Location in Africa" activity sheets

Directions
Brainstorm what a globe is while displaying one (or various kinds, ie., inflatable, with axis-inclined base, removable from stand, lighted). Have students speculate how globes are made into maps. Define and examine distortion. Discuss hemispheres and how latitude and longitude identify absolute location. Examine some map projections with Africa centered, as illustrated on the first page of the student activity sheet and/or in atlases or reference books. Guide students' reading on the first page of the activity sheets, completing the scavenger hunt next.

Relative Location in Africa

Absolute location is specific; relative location is more general. In giving descriptions of Africa's location, one must consider its place and what ordinary features are found in this region. Relative location pinpoints a particular location in relation to its surroundings.

Relative location can be used to describe Africa's major population centers. These can easily be described in various categories—inland or coastal, national capital or not, northern or southern, eastern or western.

Materials: atlases or other reference books, pencils, "Relative Location in Africa" activity sheet

Directions
Review the differences between absolute and relative location. Relate how place and region characteristics are used in describing relative location. Complete the "Relative Location in Africa" activity sheet.

Absolute Location in Africa

A *globe* is a scale model of the earth. It shows the earth's shape, lands, directions, and distances in accurate proportions. But a globe is not always convenient to use. Also, globes cannot show all of the world at one glance.

Mapmakers or *cartographers* make *maps* from globes to better display the earth. However, it is not easy or simple to make a map. Each sphere-shaped globe flattened onto a paper map loses or changes some features. This is called *distortion.*

Different maps can be projected onto paper in various ways. Computers are used to make most map projections. A map *projection* can either show accurate shapes of small areas or the correct sizes of areas, but not both. Some types of map projections are *conic, cylindrical, interrupted,* and *plane.* Africa is placed near the center of many *world* maps.

Cutting a globe in half creates *hemispheres,* halves of a sphere. Often, cartographers create their *plane projections* by cutting the earth at the equator. This represents what is often called the Northern Hemisphere (or land hemisphere) and the Southern Hemisphere (or water hemisphere). Africa is crossed by the equator, so the continent is in both the Northern and Southern Hemispheres.

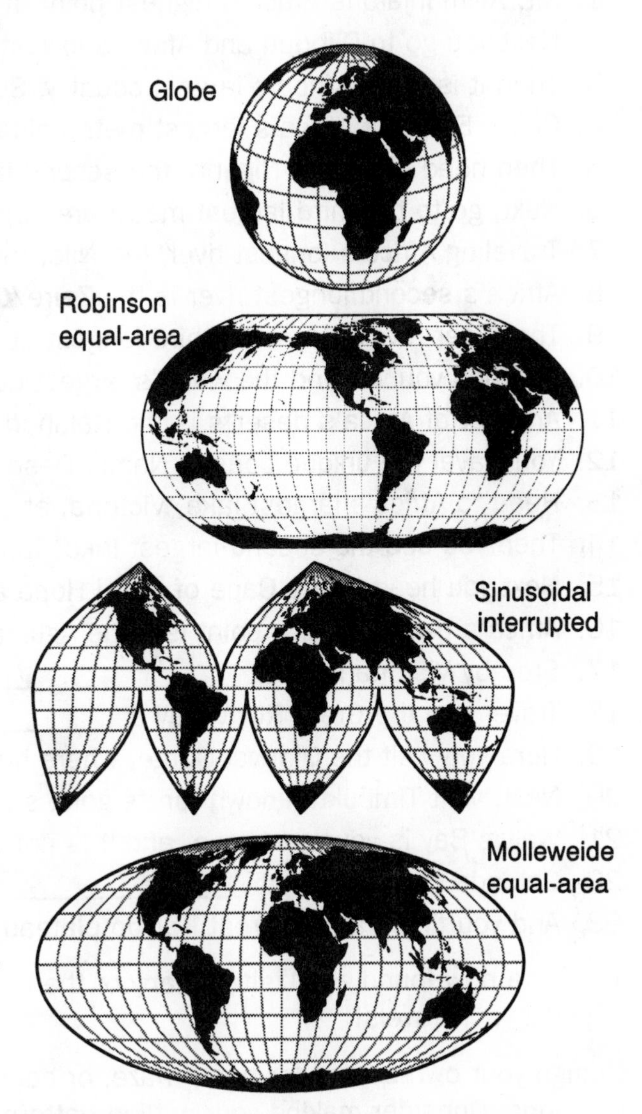

Some mapmakers cut a globe vertically through the Atlantic and Pacific Oceans, and the Arctic Ocean and Antarctica, creating the Eastern and Western Hemispheres (usually at 20°W and 160°E). This places Africa into the Eastern Hemisphere. If the prime meridian is used to cut the earth, some of western Africa (parts of Algeria through Mali, Burkina Faso, and Ghana) is found in the Western Hemisphere, and the remainder of the African continent becomes part of the Eastern Hemisphere.

The equator and prime meridian actually intersect in the Gulf of Guinea, south of Ghana and west of Gabon. This means that the African region is the only one that is found in all four directional hemispheres—Northern, Southern, Western, and Eastern. Using *latitude* with the equator and *longitude* with the prime meridian helps to identify the *absolute location* of places on maps and globes. Directions north and south of the equator and west and east of the prime meridian provide specific coordinates for any location.

Name ______________________________

Use an atlas to conduct a scavenger hunt across Africa. As you travel, identify the absolute location for each of these natural features.

1. Mt. Kilimanjaro is Africa's highest point. It is located at __________°S __________°E.
2. Next you go to Djibouti and Africa's lowest point, Lake Assal, at______________.
3. Then it is on to Africa's largest country, Sudan, and its capital, Khartoum, at ________.
4. Cairo, Egypt, is Africa's largest metropolitan area, located at ______________.
5. Then head to Lagos, Nigeria, the second largest metropolitan area, at __________.
6. Next, go to the third largest metro area of Kinshasa, Zaire, at ____________.
7. Traveling Africa's longest river, the Nile, takes you through Lake Nasser at ________.
8. Africa's second longest river is the Zaire/Congo at ____________________.
9. The Niger River is Africa's third longest at ________________________.
10. In Africa you will find the world's largest desert, the Sahara, at ____________.
11. Another of Africa's deserts is the Kalahari, where you meet the San people at _____.
12. You travel the unique coastal Namib Desert at ____________________.
13. Head to Africa's largest lake, Victoria, at __________________________.
14. Then you see the second largest lake, Tanganyika, at ________________.
15. Next you head to the Cape of Good Hope at ______________________.
16. Africa's truly southern point is Cape Agulhas at ____________________.
17. Stop by Victoria Falls at ______________________________ on the Zambezi River.
18. Travel into the Great Rift Valley at ____________________________.
19. Here you visit the Olduvai Gorge, where humans first walked this continent, at _____.
20. Next, visit Timbuktu known for its gold, salt, and slave trading at ____________.
21. Walvis Bay is your next stop, and it is not a body of water, at ____________.
22. Cabinda comes next at _____________________, with its rich oil fields for Angola.
23. And you finish at the Great Karroo plateau at ____________________.

You have now found and visited many of the outstanding locations of Africa. Hope you enjoyed your travels!

Design your own scavenger hunt, maze, or board game using some of Africa's absolute locations. Consider making your outline pattern based on African facts you have learned.

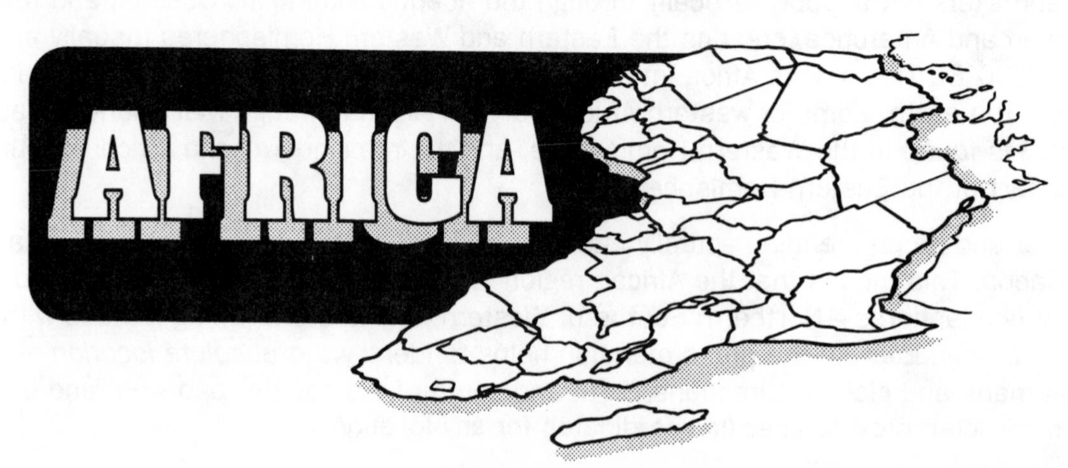

Name ______________________________

Relative Location in Africa

Africa is a huge, plateau continent with about one fifth of the earth's land surface. It is positioned across the equator, creating variable precipitation and low-fertility soils that cause environmental problems for farming and population distribution. Rich in raw materials and with less than one tenth of the world's population, Africa has great potential.

Listed below are the ten most *populous* cities in Africa. Locate each on the map.

Cairo, Egypt
Lagos, Nigeria
Kinshasa, Zaire
Casablanca, Morocco
Alexandria, Egypt
Abidjan, Cote D'Ivoire
Cape Town, South Africa
Dakar, Senegal
Addis Ababa, Ethiopia
Algiers, Algeria

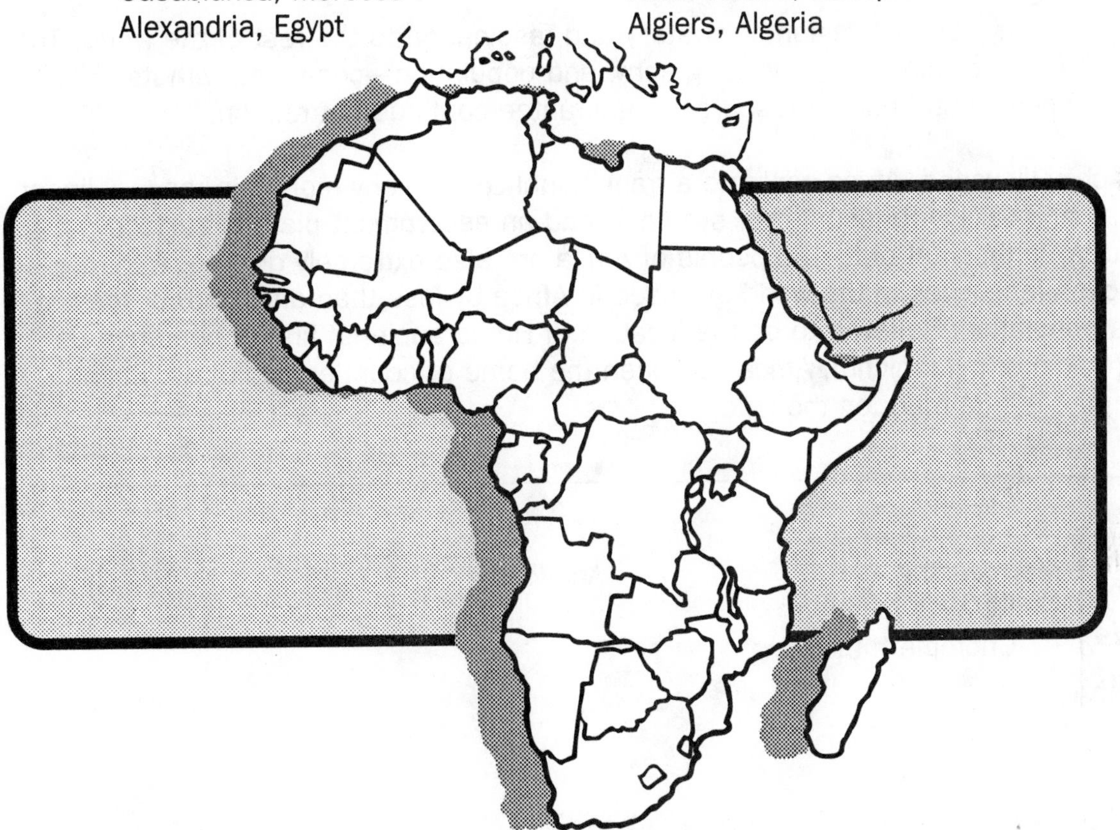

Answer the following questions. As you do, you will be using relative location, that is, using descriptive words and phrases to identify a place.

1. Describe where the most populous African cities are located. ______________________
2. Which country or region contains the most cities? ______________________
3. Are the majority in coastal or inland locations? ______________________
4. Are any of these cities the capitals of their country? ______________________
5. Why would so many Africans choose to live in these cities? ______________________

How Is Africa Unique?

Themes of Geography: *Location, Place, Region*

Objectives

Students will
1. examine physiological extremes of Africa
2. investigate and map African diversity through languages and colonization

Rationale

Africa has always been a region of mystery and fascination to the rest of the world. The appeal of Africa's unique history, geography, and population—combined with its many natural resources and human resources—guarantee continued attraction.

Geographically varied, Africa contains a transitional zone, many mountain ranges, linear rift lakes and valleys, unusual river systems, and an escarpment plateau surface created by continental drift. The people of Africa are also extremely diverse. A third of the spoken languages in the world are used in Africa by less than one tenth of the world's population. Believed to be the location of Homo sapiens' first appearance on earth (cradle of humankind), Africa has been the home of countless cultures. Each culture has left its mark on the land.

Skills Taught in This Unit

Map reading
- Relative location
- Choropleth mapping

Analysis

Vocabulary

plateaus
waterfalls
Sahel
island
peninsulas
mineral
escarpments
volcano
steppes
basins
tropical
crops
Sahara
rift valleys
rain forests
lakes
elevation
rivers
transitional
savannas
inlets
water

Physical Place Characteristics in Africa

Africa spans the Tropic of Cancer, the equator, and the Tropic of Capricorn. This unique location results in a wide variation of climate and natural regions. Situated in the center of the world's land masses, Africa is connected to Asia by a 100-mile strip of land. Furthermore, Africa is only nine miles from Europe. Although surrounded by water on three sides, Africa's location has made it accessible to and influenced by almost every major civilization in the world's history.

An acrostic puzzle allows several key words or phrases to be emphasized in a visual format that readily meets the needs of many students. Make certain that students know that not all the italicized vocabulary words are used in the puzzle.

Materials: "Physical Place Characteristics in Africa" activity sheet, pencils

Directions
Guide students' reading on the activity sheet. Discuss the vocabulary words and the features that make up the physical characteristics of a place. Students complete the acrostic puzzle, using the key words italicized in the reading.

Human Place Characteristics in Africa

One of the keys to understanding any place and its culture is language. Whether spoken, written, seen, or felt, humans have a capability which distinguishes them from all other creatures—the ability to use diverse communication methods. The wealth of languages, many with sounds and influences found only in Africa, offers a perfect opportunity for focusing on a basic human characteristic. Most African nations have at least one official language and a variety of dialects and other spoken languages.

Choropleth maps are maps that use color to provide the desired information. Some choropleth maps can show ranges of information, while others show exclusive differences.

Materials: "Human Place Characteristics in Africa" activity sheet, outline political map of Africa, colored pencils (or markers or crayons)

Directions
Discuss language as a basic part of a place's human characteristics. Guide students' reading on the activity sheet. Describe choropleth maps as those showing information using color for the key/legend. Students design a choropleth map of African languages. Examine the colonial influences of European nations on these languages, many of which are the official ones, spoken in African countries today.

Name ______________________

Physical Place Characteristics in Africa

After reading the following, identify the main characteristics that describe the physical features of Africa (the vocabulary words in italics) and place them into the acrostic puzzle—"Africa's physical place." Not all the italicized words are used in the puzzle.

Africa is a place of many unique physical characteristics. It is at the center of the earth's land masses and spans the equator. With *plateaus* and *escarpments*, the world's greatest desert (*Sahara*), and some of its strongest *rivers* and most spectacular *waterfalls*, there are also isolated snow-capped *volcanoes*, lake-filled *rift valleys*, and a *transitional* zone called the *Sahel*. There are scorched *steppes* and luscious *rain forests*; there are overgrazed *savannas* and isolated *island* realms (such as Madagascar, the world's fourth largest island).

What Africa does not have is a long mountain range. Nor do the rivers flow in regular courses. The plateau surface is not unbroken and flat. The Sahara is not all sand, and the *basins* (Chad, Djouf, Kalahari, Sudan, and Zaire/Congo) are no longer great inland seas or *lakes*. Few *inlets* and *peninsulas* exist.

```
      _ _ A _ _ _ _ _
  _ _ _ _ f _ _ _ _ _ _
  _ _ _ _ r _ _ _ _ _
        _ i _ _ _ _
    _ _ _ c _ _ _ _ _
        _ a _ _ _
        _ s _ _ _ _

    _ _ _ p _ _ _
      _ _ h _ _ _
_ _ _ _   _ _ _ _ _ y _
      _ _ s _ _ _
    _ _ _ i _ _ _ _ _ _
_ _ _ _ _ c _ _
    _ _ _ a _ _ _ _
_ _ _ _ _ _ l

    _ _ _ p _
      _ _ l _ _ _
        _ a _ _ _
      _ _ c _ _ _ _ _ _ _ _
    _ _ _ e _
```

About 80 percent of Africa lies in *tropical* climates. *Elevation*, daily temperature changes, varying amounts of rainfall, and seasonal winds create climate diversity and influence the economy of Africa.

Another factor that affects the physical traits of Africa is the abundance of resources. *Water* and *mineral* resources, including copper, diamonds, gold, iron, manganese, uranium, coal, and petroleum, provide Africa with great potential.

Tropical *crops* also contribute to Africa's economy. These include cacao, coffee, palm oil, rubber, and timber. But the vast majority of crops are of the subsistence variety (maize, manioc, millet, cassava, sorghum) that farmers grow to feed themselves.

Human Place Characteristics in Africa

Language is one trait humans give a place. It is the key to communication. By most accounts, there are 800 to 1,000 languages spoken throughout Africa. This number does not include the many dialects within these languages. In some nations, such as Nigeria, more than 250 dialects are spoken. There are over 400 different Bantu languages. Bantu-speaking people form the largest ethnic language group in Africa. As a result of migrating, trading, and colonizing, ethnic groups have blended together. There are European languages spoken, especially French and English, showing the influence colonization had on Africa. Blending people together creates new languages.

Design a choropleth map with the following colors to symbolize the languages spoken and the European influence within Africa. Official languages are italicized.

French = red	English = blue	Portuguese = orange
Spanish = yellow	Arabic = green	Swahili = brown

Algeria: *Arabic*, French, Berber
Angola: *Portuguese*, Bantu, Ovimbundo
Benin: *French*, Yon, Yoruba
Botswana: *English*, Setswana
Burkina Faso: *French*
Burundi: *Kirundi, French*, Swahili
Cameroon: *English, French*
Cape Verde, *Portuguese*, Criolo
Central African Republic: *French*, Sangho
Chad: French, *Arabic*, Sara
Comoros: *Arabic, French*, Comoran
Congo: *French*, Lingala, Kikongo
Cote D'Ivoire: *French*, Dioula
Djibouti: *French, Arabic*, Somali, Afar
Egypt: *Arabic*, English, French
Equatorial Guinea: *Spanish*, pidgin English
Eritrea: *Tigre*, Kunama, Arabic
Ethiopia: *Amharic*, Arabic, English
Gabon: *French*, Fang, Myene
Gambia: *English*, Mandinka, Wolof
Ghana: *English*, Akan, Ewe, Ga
Guinea: *French*
Guinea-Bissau: *Portuguese*, Criolo
Kenya: *English, Swahili*
Lesotho: *Sesotho, English*, Zulu, Xhosa
Liberia: *English*, Niger-Congo dialects
Libya: *Arabic*, Italian, English
Madagascar: *French, Malagasy*
Malawi: *English, Chichewa*
Mali: *French*, Bambara
Mauritania: *Arabic, Wolof,* French
Mauritius: *English*, Creole, Hindi
Morocco: *Arabic*, Berber
Mozambique: *Portuguese*
Namibia: *English*, Afrikaans, German
Niger: *French*, Hausa, Djerma
Nigeria: *English*, Hausa, Yoruba, Ibo
Rwanda: *Kinyarwanda*, French
Sao Tome & Principe: *Portuguese*
Senegal: *French*, Wolof, Pular
Seychelles: *English, French*, Creole
Sierra Leone: *English*, Mende, Temne
Somalia: *Somali*, Arabic, Italian
South Africa: *Afrikaans, English*, Zulu
Sudan: *Arabic*, Nubian, English
Swaziland: *English, siSwati*
Tanzania: *Swahili*, English
Togo: *French*, Ewe, Mina, Dagomba
Tunisia: *Arabic*, French
Uganda: *English*, Swahili, Bantu
Western Sahara: *Arabic*
Zaire: *French*, Lingala, Swahili
Zambia: *English*, Nyanja, Bamba
Zimbabwe: *English*, Shona, Sindebele

Explain which languages (colors) are dominant on your map. Which regions of Africa were mainly colonized by the French? The English? In which region is Arabic spoken? How did languages spread across Africa?

Africa

How Does Interaction Affect Africa?

Themes of Geography: *Location, Place, Interaction, Movement, Region*

Objectives

Students will

1. examine and analyze health in Africa
2. map "AIDS Belt" in Africa
3. speculate and propose solutions on desertification in Africa

Rationale

Africa suffers from low life expectancies, high infant mortality, local and regional famines, poor nutrition, and diseases. Endemic and pandemic diseases are related to Africa's physical geography. AIDS (Acquired Immune Deficiency Syndrome) first appeared in blood collected in 1959 in Central Africa. AIDS was not formally identified until 1981 but has become a modern pandemic. Spread chiefly by sexual contact, intravenous drug use, and transfusion of infected blood, it mainly strikes young and middle-aged adults. The economic, political, and social losses caused by health problems cause serious concerns for many African nations.

One of the world's major environmental concerns is *desertification*. In recent years, significant shortage of rainfall has led to widespread drought. Drought is endemic to the Sahel region of Africa. Drought, the pressures of population, and poor land management techniques (overgrazing, devegetation, soil degradation, cutting and burning of trees, and overcultivation) have caused the desert to shift southward at a rate of two to six miles per year. Famines are also caused by desertification.

Skills Taught in This Unit

Map reading
- Relative location

Analysis

Vocabulary

life expectancy	*infant mortality*	*famine*	*deficiency*
subsistence farming	*malnutrition*	*drought*	*malaria*
tsetse fly	*schistosomiasis*	*parasites*	*plague*
AIDS	*HIV*	*desertification*	*reforestation*
erg	*poaching*		

Health and Diseases in Africa

Several factors cause health problems in Africa. Many diseases affect humans, animals, and plants in Africa and are a great concern. Indigenous diseases of Africa are often pandemic (spread over a large region). Epidemic diseases, such as the Ebola virus, have historically been spread by trade and war. Today, many African epidemics are spread by more physical contact over shorter periods of time.

Infant mortality and life expectancy are two statistics that reveal a lot about health in an area. Life expectancy is included in the Human Development Index (HDI), a combined set of statistics for life expectancy, adult literacy rate, and basic purchasing power formulated in 1990. It is generally easier for students to conceive of how many infants die in their first year of life or how long an individual can hope to live.

Materials: "Health and Diseases in Africa" activity sheet, pencils, outline political map of Africa

Directions
Discuss how health, especially life expectancy and infant mortality, relates to all geographic themes. Explain the factual history of AIDS (HIV). Carefully guide students' reading of the activity sheet. Have students map the "AIDS Region" in Africa and plan a solution for improving health in an African country.

Desertification in Africa

Africa is largely desert and marginal areas becoming desert—many geologists say Africa has more desert landscapes than any other continent. Desertification in Africa from overgrazing and deforestation is a major ecological concern. Deserts are one climatic region that seems to endure and grow while others dwindle and disappear over time.

Various groups offer different solutions for desertification. Strategies that have been tried in the past may continue to offer some hope. Many people feel that more aggressive methods will have to be implemented in the future and at a greater rate if Africa is to stave off the encroachment of deserts.

Materials: "Desertification in Africa" activity sheet, pencils, atlas (or other reference book)

Directions
Brainstorm the definition of *desertification*. Guide students' reading of the activity sheet. Have students present their debates.

Health and Diseases in Africa

Africa's people suffer from lower *life expectancies* than those in any other region of our world. *Infant mortality* is also quite high throughout Africa. These phenomena are caused by poor nutrition, local and regional *famines*, and diseases.

Subsistence farming of grain and root crops, along with herding animals, give many Africans just enough to feed themselves. Since their staple foods are mainly carbohydrates, many Africans are in poor health. Food-*deficiency* disorders (such as marasmus from a lack of protein) do not kill people, but they often lower their disease resistance as they age. The ownership of livestock is often seen as a sign of social status, and the animals are not used for human consumption. Many African herders face problems of traveling long distances to get animals to markets and insects that attack their herds and cause diseases.

Africans are at risk because of limited food availability. Famine and *malnutrition* have caused great suffering in recent years in Ethiopia and Sudan. Savanna areas experience *droughts* when water and vegetation are scarce, and herders also suffer with their animals during droughts. Pastures and crops are frequently destroyed by locusts.

Tropical areas of Africa are breeding areas for diseases. *Malaria*, spread by mosquitoes, is one of the worst diseases. It is found in most all areas of Africa. Many Africans suffer from malaria all their lives. Sleeping sickness, caused by the *tsetse fly*, affects people and livestock. It has traveled from tropical areas of West Africa into East Africa with the migration of cattle herders. Yellow fever, caused by a virus and transmitted by mosquitoes, is another disease which is widespread in tropical Africa. River blindness, caused by a parasitic worm carried by a fly, is found mainly in the savanna south of the Sahara. *Schistosomiasis* (or bilharzia), caused by *parasites* in snails, is not fatal, but comes from unsanitary water. *Plague*, caused by fleas, has been a problem in Africa for centuries.

Since the earliest evidence of *AIDS* (Acquired Immune Deficiency Syndrome) in Central Africa in 1959, the disease has become quite deadly to Africans. *HIV* (Human Immunodeficiency Virus)—the virus that causes AIDS—has a second strain (HIV-2), rarely found outside Africa. Over 10 percent of the population of Botswana, Burundi, Cote D'Ivoire, Kenya, Malawi, Rwanda, Tanzania, Uganda, Zambia, and Zimbabwe are HIV positive. The African "AIDS Region," where 90 percent of the cases are found, includes Burundi, Congo, Kenya, Malawi, Rwanda, Tanzania, Uganda, Zaire, Zambia, and Zimbabwe.

A study of the infant mortality rate is one of the best ways to learn about the health of a country. No African nation has an infant mortality rate lower than 50 deaths per 1,000 babies under one year of age.

Map the "AIDS Region" on an outline map of Africa. Identify each of the ten countries.

You are the Minister of Health for an African nation. Design a plan to lower infant mortality rates and increase life expectancies in your country.

Desertification in Africa

Africa contains the Sahara, the world's largest desert. It also has other great deserts, including the Kalahari and the Namib. Some of these African deserts are spreading as much as two to six miles per year.

The spread of deserts is called *desertification*. Many years of drought in Africa have made desertification a real danger for this continent. In the Sahel, south of the Sahara, Africans are being driven south as crops and pastures dry up. For African nations that have food shortages, losing cropland is a serious problem. Land has been overgrazed in many areas.

Human interaction, such as animal *poaching* and war, have contributed to desertification.

Deforestation in some areas has caused creeping sands to bury whole towns in the Sahel region. Stripping trees for fuel and clearing land for cultivation have left much of the Sahel devastated. Forests are important in climate regulation.

Another major problem is the erosion of precious topsoil by wind. Sand covers croplands and roads as the desert moves. Shifting sand dunes are called *ergs*.

In the 1980s, millions of people starved or became refugees in the Sahel, especially in Ethiopia and Sudan. The nomadic Tuaregs of Mali have been forced to settle in towns.

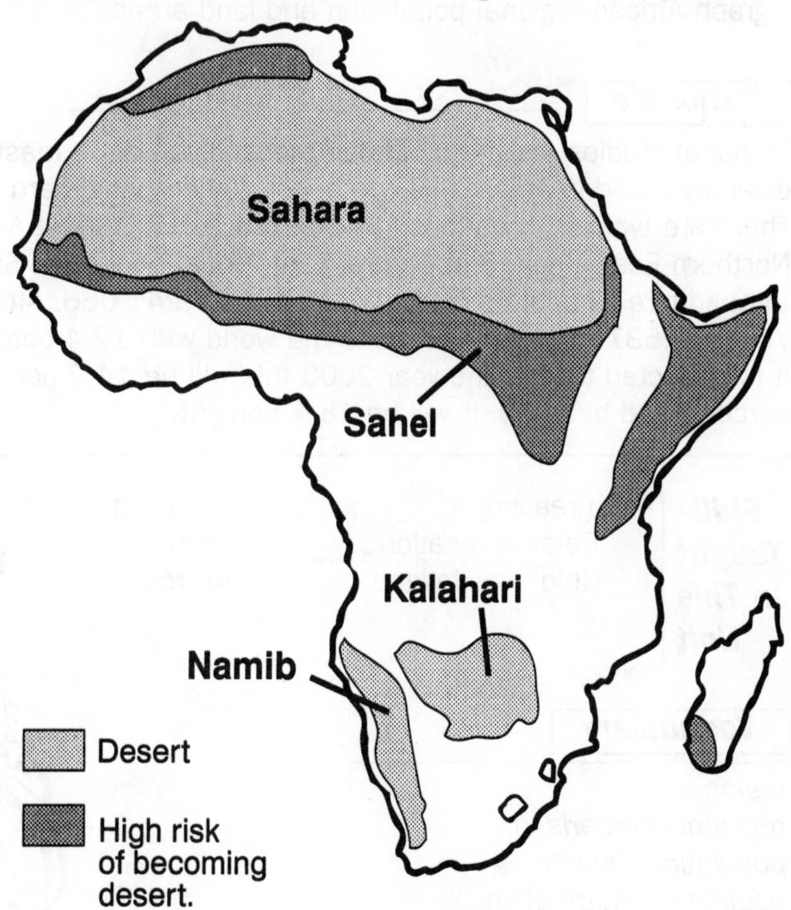

Study the map and note the areas (countries or regions) that are at risk of becoming desert.

Prepare a debate in which farmers and herders of the Sahel will debate with forestry officials and a Peace Corps Volunteer (specializing in *reforestation*) on how to live in harmony with the environment of Africa.

Africa

What Are the African Regions?

Themes of Geography: *Location, Place, Region*

Objectives

Students will
1. identify and locate regions within Africa
2. interpret regional comparisons with land area and population
3. graph African regional population and land areas

Rationale

Regional studies are the most comprehensive way to master geography. With the diversity found in Africa, this can become the springboard or finale of these studies. There are typically 6 nations in North Africa, 17 in West Africa, 7 in Central Africa, 5 in Northern East Africa, 6 in Central East Africa, and 13 in Southern Africa. Therefore, the total square kilometers found in Africa is 29,241,066. Africa's total population of 705,819,537 makes it second in the world with 12.4 percent of the world's population. It is projected that by the year 2000 this will be 14.2 percent, by 2010, it will be 15.4 percent, and by 2025, it will be 18.4 percent.

Skills Taught in This Unit

Map reading
- Relative location
- Color key/legend

Graphing
- Bar
- Circle

Vocabulary

region
regional comparison
population density
population distribution

Regions Within Africa

Africa's regions can be identified in various ways. For this unit's study, six are used: **North Africa:** Algeria, Egypt, Libya, Morocco, Tunisia, and Western Sahara.

West Africa: Benin, Burkina Faso, Cape Verde, Chad, Cote d'Ivoire, Gambia, Ghana, Guinea, Guinea-Bissau, Liberia, Mali, Mauritania, Niger, Nigeria, Senegal, Sierra Leone, and Togo.

Central Africa: Cameroon, Central African Republic, Congo, Equatorial Guinea, Gabon, Sao Tome & Principe, and Zaire.

Northern East Africa: Djiboouti, Eritrea, Ethiopia, Somalia, and Sudan.

Central East Africa: Burundi, Kenya, Rwanda, Seychelles, Tanzania, and Uganda

Southern Africa: Angola, Botswana, Comoros, Lesotho, Madagascar, Malawi, Mauritius, Mozambique, Namibia, South Africa, Swaziland, Zambia, and Zimbabwe.

Disagreements and controversies sometimes erupt in debates over which nation belongs in which region. Example: Western Sahara is not officially recognized as a nation by many other countries in the world. It is often included as part of Morocco or even Mauritania because of the unsettled status of this area in Northern Africa. Some island nations are often excluded in any regional study or placed in different regions. Example: Mauritius is often considered a part of Asia.

Population distribution in Africa's regions provides an interesting study for geography and culture. Studying population density in the various regions offers an opportunity to analyze why people choose to live in certain places. Population density is the number of people per square kilometer or square mile in a given land area.

Materials: "Regions Within Africa" activity sheet, blank outline political map of Africa, pencils, colored pencils (or markers or crayons), atlases (or other reference materials)

Directions
Define *region*. Guide students' reading, mapping, and graphing of the activity sheet. Discuss projected population increases for Africa over the next two decades. What impact will these population growths have on this continent and its regions?

Name ______________________

Regions Within Africa

Africa is generally divided into geographical regions: north, west, central, northern east, central east, and southern.

The six nations usually included in North Africa are Algeria, Egypt, Libya, Morocco, Tunisia, and Western Sahara. West Africa includes Benin, Burkina Faso, Cape Verde, Chad, Cote d'Ivoire, Gambia, Ghana, Guinea, Guinea-Bissau, Liberia, Mali, Mauritania, Niger, Nigeria, Senegal, Sierra Leone, and Togo. Seven nations are considered part of Central Africa: Cameroon, Central African Republic, Congo, Equatorial Guinea, Gabon, Sao Tome and Principe, and Zaire. Northern East Africa contains Djibouti, Eritrea, Ethiopia, Somalia, and Sudan. Central East Africa includes Burundi, Kenya, Rwanda, Seychelles, Tanzania, and Uganda. Angola, Botswana, Comoros, Lesotho, Madagascar, Malawi, Mauritius, Mozambique, Namibia, South Africa, Swaziland, Zambia, and Zimbabwe are in Southern Africa.

On the map of Africa, use this key to color the countries to show in which region they belong.

north = green	west = red	central = yellow
northern east = blue	central east = orange	southern = purple

Do a *regional comparison* of Africa's *regions*, their land area, and population.

Region	Land Area sq. km.	Population	Population sq. km.	Population by Region
North Africa	6,019,660	130,646,944	21.70 people	18.5%
West Africa	6,311,724	200,972,352	31.84 people	28.5%
Northern East African	4,414,227	97,992,122	22.20 people	13.9%
Central East African	1,818,405	91,318,878	50.22 people	12.9%
Central Africa	4,082,514	63,019,087	15.44 people	8.9%
Southern Africa	6,594,530	121,870,435	18.48 people	17.3%

1. Which African region has the greatest land area? Which has the smallest?

   ____

2. Which African region has the largest population? Which has the smallest?

   ____

3. Design a bar graph showing *population density* for each African region.
4. Design a circle graph showing the percentage of population for each African region (population distribution).

Regions of Africa

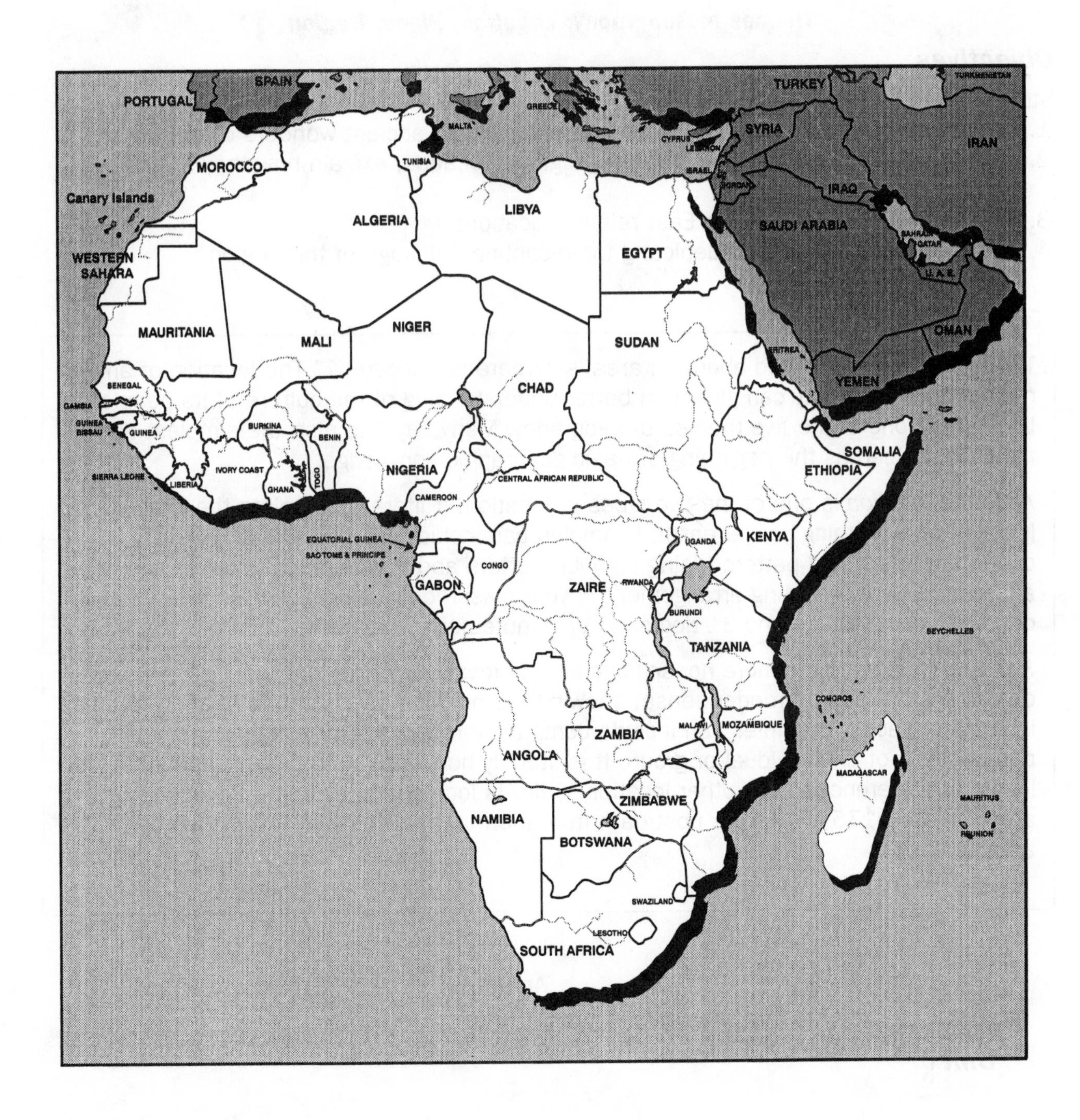

North Africa/Middle East

Where Is North Africa/Middle East?

Themes of Geography: *Location, Place, Region*

Objectives

Students will

1. use atlases and maps to identify absolute location of ancient wonders of the world
2. identify on a map places having strategic global location; explain how they affect political decisions
3. describe North Africa/Middle East relative locations
4. draw a triple Venn diagram depicting three-continent linkage of this region

Rationale

The initial question asked about an area is "Where is it located?" The location of any region, country, or city can give us a better understanding of the culture of its people. Location is one of the five themes of geography. Many say it is also the simplest and must be studied as the beginning of basic geographic knowledge.

Absolute location is one of the two types of location. It literally pinpoints the exact location of everything on the earth. Examples can include latitude and longitude coordinates, any grid pattern (using alphabet letters and numbers on its axes), an address, even the seating arrangement in your classroom. Cairo, Egypt, is located at 30 degrees north latitude and 31 degrees, 17 minutes east longitude.

Relative location is the more nonspecific kind of location. Words are most often used to describe a place in a broader sense, showing the position of an area in relation to other important places. Examples can include compass directions, time/distance, or perspectives of an individual or group. It is literally how one relates where something is located in reference to any other location. Cairo is located in northeast Egypt, approximately 175 kilometers upstream from the mouth of the Nile River in its delta area.

Skills Taught in This Unit

Map reading
- Latitude and longitude
- Relative location

Analysis

Expository writing

Vocabulary

absolute location *relative location* *region*

Absolute Location in North Africa/Middle East

Sometimes North Africa is studied with the African continent, and the Middle East (or Southwest Asia) is studied with the Asian continent. Many geographers consider it a single region and prefer that it be studied this way.

Materials: atlases or other reference books, pencils, "Absolute Location in North Africa/Middle East" activity sheets, paper (or computer)

Directions
Brainstorm the definition of *location* with students. Discuss the concept of absolute location and how to use latitude and longitude to find the location of a city or natural feature. Guide students' reading on the first page of the activity. Distribute atlases and other reference materials for students to use while identifying and locating the ancient wonders of the world. Students may work independently or as partners. Identify, using atlases or other reference books, strategic locations in North Africa/Middle East, such as the Turkish Straits (Dardanelles, Sea of Marmara, Bosporus), the Suez Canal, the Strait of Hormuz/Musandam Peninsula, and the Strait of Gibraltar.

Relative Location in North Africa/Middle East

North Africa/Middle East is considered by geographers to be an important crossroads region that serves as a connection between continents and major bodies of water.

Materials: atlases or other reference books; student activity sheets; three Hoola-Hoops (or chalk circles drawn on outdoor surface or noncarpeted floor or yarn circles on carpet); placards labeled "Africa," "Asia," "Europe"; "Relative Location of North Africa/Middle East" activity sheet cut and glued or taped onto cards

Directions
Carefully guide students' reading on the first activity sheet. Using atlases or other reference books, students describe solutions for relative location scenarios posed on the second sheet. Place Hoola-Hoops (chalk or yarn circles) intersecting as a triple Venn diagram on the floor (ground). Place one placard each for Africa, Asia, and Europe into the center of each circle. Discuss how these three continents are linked in this region. Have student representatives holding description cards stand in the correct Venn diagram locations. (Egypt will need to straddle Africa and Asia, just as Turkey will need to straddle Asia and Europe.) Discuss the implications of relative location on countries in the Middle East, ie., which people are Arab but do not live in Africa, Asia, or even Europe; which country is arid/dry; which country is possibly more Asian than African. Reinforcement of place and region should be discussed to connect geographic themes.

a. Describe some of the human and physical characteristics of the Middle East.
b. Explain where this region gets its nicknames.
c. Discuss how location, place, and regions are related.

Absolute Location in North Africa/Middle East

Northern Africa and the Middle East are studied as one *region* in this unit. The slender link of the Sinai Peninsula and the water crossroads provided by the Mediterranean and Red Seas bond the people of Northern Africa and the Middle East in a relationship that has existed from the beginning of history.

- North Africa includes Morocco, Algeria, Libya, Egypt, Tunisia, Western Sahara, and the northeastern portion of Sudan. The Sahara Desert divides Africa into the northern and southern regions. North Africa is north of the Sahara. With an ocean of sand at its back, and the Atlantic Ocean, Mediterranean Sea, and Red Sea providing its other borders, Northern Africa's principal land route crosses the Sinai Peninsula to the Middle East.
- The Middle East includes Turkey, Cyprus, Iran, Afghanistan, Saudi Arabia, Yemen, Oman, United Arab Emirates, Qatar, Bahrain, Kuwait, Iraq, Syria, Jordan, and Israel. The Middle East is literally in the middle of the Eastern Hemisphere. Europe is west of these countries; Asia is east.

Most of the seven ancient wonders of the world were located within ancient North Africa and the Middle East. These included the following:

1. Egyptian Pyramids at Giza
2. Hanging Gardens of Babylon
3. Lighthouse at Alexandria
4. Statue of Zeus at Olympia
5. Colossus of Rhodes
6. Temple of Artemis at Ephesus
7. Mausoleum at Halicarnassus.

Some of the locations of these ancient wonders are difficult to find today. Babylon and Halicarnassus no longer exist, Constantinople is now Istanbul, and Ephesus is now near Sulcuk. Here are the *absolute locations* for some of these:

		Latitude	Longitude
Hanging Gardens	Babylon	32°N	45°E
Statue of Zeus	Constantinople	41°N	29°E
Colossus	Rhodes	36°N	28 E
Temple of Artemis	Ephesus	38°N	27°E
Mausoleum	Halicarnassus	36°N	27°E

Locate these *absolute location* coordinates on the map. Label each by its place name.

Name ____________________

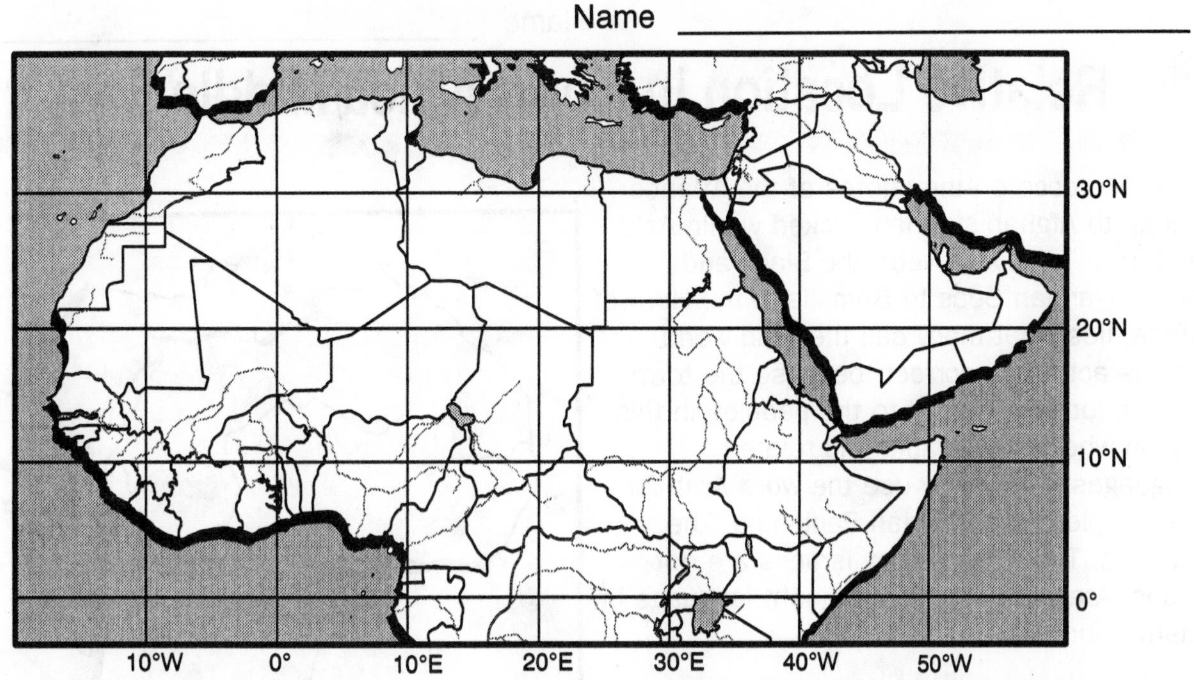

Use an atlas to find Giza (which is a suburb of Cairo) and Alexandria in Egypt. Give their absolute locations:

Giza (Cairo), Egypt ____________________

Alexandria, Egypt ____________________

Use an atlas to answer the following questions about the locations of the ancient wonders of the world:

1. The present-day country of ________________ would be where the Hanging Gardens were located along the banks of the __________ River.
2. Constantinople is now called ____________. It is now located in ________ on the Sea of __________ leading into the __________ Strait.
3. Rhodes would be in ____________, on the coast of the _________ Sea.
4. Ephesus would be near the present town of Sulcuk on the southwest coast of _______.
5. The tomb of Mausolus in Asia Minor would be in the present-day country of ________.
6. Alexandria is located on the coast of the ___________ Sea.
7. Cairo and Giza are located along the ____________ River.

Use an atlas to locate and identify the following strategic locations on your map:

Dardanelles
Bosporous Strait
Strait of Hormuz
Sea of Marmara
Suez Canal
Musandam Peninsula
Strait of Gibraltar

Write an expository paragraph telling how these locations could affect political decisions made by governments in this region.

Name ______________________

Relative Location in North Africa/Middle East

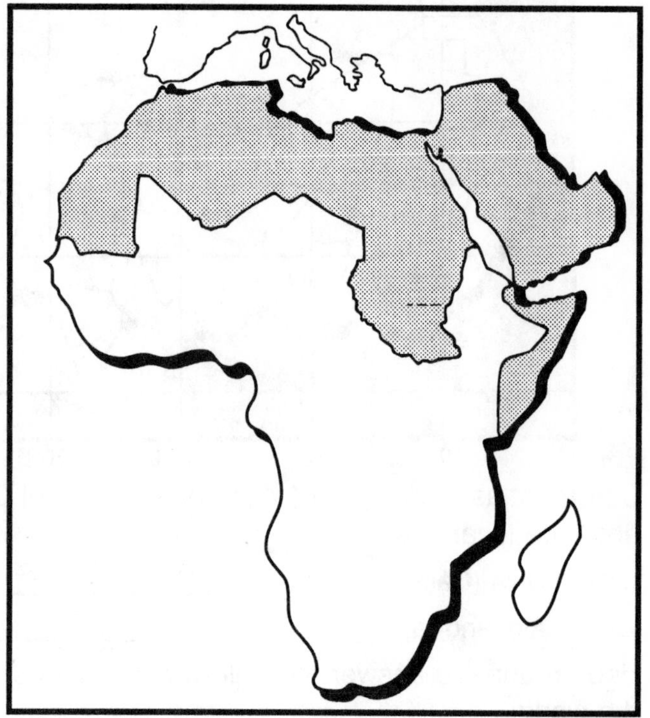

From Morocco on the shores of the Atlantic Ocean to Afghanistan landlocked within Asia, and from Turkey between the Black and Mediterranean Seas to Somalia in the Horn of Africa, lies what many call the Arab world. This is actually incorrect, because the term *Arab* is loosely applied to the peoples in this region who speak Arabic and related languages. Many only use the word *Arab* for the people of the Arabian Peninsula. The Iranians, Turks, and many Israelis are not Arabs. Arabic is not the dominant language in many countries.

Another name often given to the North Africa/Middle East region is "World of Islam." This terminology is also incorrect. Many people in the region practice Judaism and Christianity, including Coptic Christians. The largest Islamic population of any nation in the world, Indonesia, is not even in this region. Indonesia is in Southeast Asia.

"Dry World" is another name given to this region. Though the desert climate dominates this region, many areas have access to water from rivers, seas, gulfs, and precipitation. Water as a permanent resource is a major concern. However, with traditional techniques and modern technology, water does exist in this dry land.

This region is also referred to as the crossroads of the world. The Sinai Peninsula acts as a land bridge connecting Africa to Asia. The Mediterranean Sea acts as a water link connecting Africa, Europe, and Asia. The Suez Canal links the Mediterranean Sea to the Red Sea, which provides another crossroads for transportation and travel.

The best nickname is Middle East. It is not a perfect description, but at least it shows the important role this region has in linking three continents. The intersection of Africa, Asia, and Europe can be found in the middle, or the Middle East.

Name ______________________

Relative Location in North Africa/Middle East

The following *relative location* descriptions can be completed using an atlas.

1. This nation is largely Asian. It includes the Anatolia plateau. The western peninsula contains Istanbul, the largest city (that once was Constantinople)—the only city in the world on two continents. The country is about twice the size of California and is European and Asian. The strategic locations of the straits, Bosporus and Dardanelles, as well as the Black Sea and Mediterranean Sea give this nation many advantages. It is also the source for the Tigris and Euphrates Rivers. WHAT COUNTRY IS THIS? ______________

---

2. The Sinai Peninsula is in this country. Through it, this country connects Africa and Asia. It also has the Suez Canal and Nile River to supply it with water and income. Parts of the Sahara—the Arabian, Libyan, and Nubian Deserts—cover much of its landscape. It is about the size of Texas, Oklahoma, and Arkansas combined.
   WHAT COUNTRY IS THIS? ______________________________

---

3. Many describe this nation as the climate crossroads of the world. It has the Negev Desert, the Jordan River, the Dead Sea, and the Sea of Galilee, which create climate diversity. The flora and fauna found here represent those found in Europe, Asia, and Africa. This country is about the size of New Jersey.
   WHAT COUNTRY IS THIS? ______________________________

---

4. Many call this nation's great desert the "Empty Quarter"; to Arabic speakers it is the *Rub al Khali*. This country is one third the size of the United States. The Red Sea and Persian Gulf form this country's western and eastern borders. It is the core of the peninsula that shares part of its name. WHAT IS THIS COUNTRY? ______________

---

5. The smallest of the nations in this region encompasses 35 sand-covered islands located in the Persian Gulf. Only six of these islands are inhabited. Causeways link this island nation with two other islands and Saudi Arabia's mainland. It is smaller than New York City. WHAT IS THIS COUNTRY? ______________________

---

6. Africa is closest to Europe at this nation's northern tip. Spain is only nine miles across the Strait of Gibraltar. This nation is larger than California. It is known as the Far West in the Arab countries of northwest Africa called the *Maghreb*—which means "west." It also claims Western Sahara as part of its territory; however, a vote to settle the dispute over this claim has been prevented from taking place.
   WHAT COUNTRY IS THIS? ______________________________

---

7. In the extreme eastern edge of this region is a nation about the size of Texas that is often studied with South Asia. The Khyber Pass, which became the link between Southwest and South Asia, caused this country to be called the "crossroads of Central Asia." A landlocked nation covered with mountains and desert, this nation has been invaded numerous times, resulting in ethnic and tribal diversity.
   WHAT IS THIS COUNTRY? ______________________________

How Is North Africa/Middle East Unique?

Themes of Geography: *Location, Place, Movement, Interaction, Region*

Objectives

Students will
1. examine water and riverine civilizations
2. describe surface features of the Sahara
3. analyze culture, emphasizing religious and political systems
4. justify viewpoint on government types

Rationale

Physical traits of this region revolve around the land and lack of water. Water is of vital importance and a constant cause of concern. Historical, cultural, economic, and physical geography are all woven into the landscape.

Human place characteristics include many aspects of culture—art, architecture, ethnic foods, economy, fashion, government, language, literature, occupations, religion, recreation, and tradition. This study of North Africa/Middle East focuses on religion and government, as this region is noted for being the spiritual center or birthplace of three of the world's great religions and for being a part of the world plagued by constant political discord.

Skills Taught in This Unit

Map reading	Composition	Analysis
Relative location	Descriptive writing	

Vocabulary

oasis	*exotic*	*culture hearths*	*erg*
aquifer	*tributary*	*Fertile Crescent*	*hammada*
qanat	*riverine civilizations*	*Torah*	*reg*
wadi	*Palestine*	*Arabia*	*Judaism*
Christianity	*Islam*	*Muslim*	*deity*
prophet	*monotheism*	*afterlife*	*ethnic group*
sharia	*parliamentary*	*mosque*	*minaret*
arabesque	*calligraphy*	*Menorah*	
crucifix	*kosher*		

Physical Place Characteristics in North Africa/Middle East

The arid land and the necessary water of North Africa and the Middle East make this region's physical place characteristics some of the most misunderstood in the world. Dilemmas and conflicts have arisen over many centuries among many cultures to name, to share, and to have these lands and waters.

Materials: "Physical Place Characteristics in North Africa/Middle East" activity sheet, pencil, dictionary, string, glue

Directions
Discuss why most maps and globes show land colors in shades of green and brown. Guide students' reading and answering on the activity sheet.

Human Place Characteristics in North Africa/Middle East

In understanding the human qualities of this region, the study of the religion/belief system becomes very important. Probably nowhere else in the world will we find the historical importance and political influence that theology places on this region.

Many aspects of human place characteristics, such as art, architecture, language, diet, and clothing, can be incorporated into the study of a region's beliefs and political systems. By drawing parallels between these place characteristics, students can grasp an overall understanding of any region.

Materials: "Human Place Characteristics in North Africa/Middle East" activity sheets, pencil

Directions
Guide students' reading of the activity sheet with an emphasis on vocabulary. Students complete the written assignment, making certain they can substantiate their interpretations of the government types.

Name ____________________

Physical Place Characteristics in North Africa/Middle East

The water in the North Africa/Middle East region creates a landscape of green and brown. In some places, water is so scarce it is sold by the glass or pitcher. The importance of a green oasis, an *aquifer*, a *qanat* (an underground tunnel), or a river valley offers proof that water is essential for life. Traditional and modern techniques are used to bring water to the brown land. Farmers, nomads and their herds, and urban dwellers all inhabit this region where water is available.

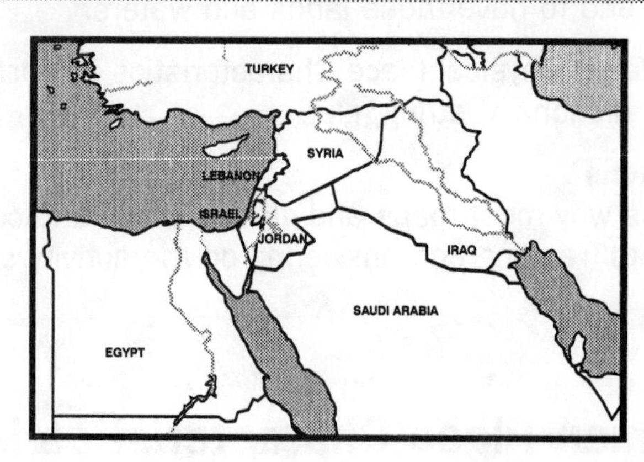

Exotic rivers get their names because they flow continually across deserts, which is unusual. The Nile River and Tigris and Euphrates Rivers are two of the exotic river systems in this region. The *tributaries* of the Nile (the Blue, White, and Atbara), the Jordan River, and the Helmond River are also important water sources of the region.

Egypt is often called "the gift of the Nile," while Mesopotamia (mainly Iran today) where the Tigris and Euphrates flow is called "the land between the two rivers." These two *riverine civilizations* are part of the *culture hearths* found in the Eastern Hemisphere and make up the *Fertile Crescent*.

Sahara is an Arabic word meaning "wilderness" or "desert." This is why Sahara is often used without the name "desert" attached to it. The landscape of a desert can contain *ergs* (shifting sand dunes), *hammadas* (rocky plateaus surrounding oases), *regs* (plains covered with gravel and sand), and *wadis* (dry river valleys with flat bottoms). An *oasis* is a green, fertile place in the desert that has a water supply.

The Syrian Desert and the *Rub-al-Khali*, or "Empty Quarter," are two other deserts found in this region. Saudi Arabia's Rub-al-Khali is a huge erg desert, and its capital, Riyadh, was founded around a large oasis.

1. Define *aquifer*. ____________________
2. An ____________ river is unusual because it flows continually across a desert.
3. How do the nicknames "gift of the Nile" and "land between the two rivers" relate to the Fertile Crescent? ____________________
4. Identify five surface features found in the Sahara. ____________________
5. Define *Sahara* and *Rub-al-Khali*. ____________________
6. Glue a piece of string onto the map in a crescent shape where the Fertile Crescent would be located.

Human Place Characteristics in North Africa/Middle East

There is a close connection between religion and culture in North Africa/Middle East. Religion influences architecture, art, fashion, and government, and many other aspects of culture.

Three of the world's great religions originated in North Africa/Middle East and the Southwest Asia region. In the areas of ancient *Palestine* and *Arabia, Judaism, Christianity,* and *Islam* began. The oldest is Judaism, with Christianity growing out of Judaism. Islam brought together parts of Judaism and Christianity in the seventh century A.D. These faiths share several common factors, such as a belief in one *deity* (*monotheism*), a belief in many of the same *prophets*, and a belief in an *afterlife*. People of all three religions believe that Jerusalem is a holy place.

Arabs are the largest *ethnic group* in this region. They are united by their language, Arabic, and by their religions. Most Arabs are *Muslims* practicing Islam, but there are also Jewish and Christian Arabs. Non-Arab people, especially in Turkey and Iran, share Islam but not the Arabic language and some other customs.

Many governments in this region live by *sharia*, Islamic law. Iran is an example of a country in which religious leaders depend on sharia and are also important in its government. Several nations have different styles of democratic or free political systems. Saudi Arabia is greatly influenced by Islam, but it blends sharia with western law. Israel's laws are affected by Jewish law, and it has a *parliamentary* government system. Turkey is a democracy found in a mostly Muslim nation.

Architecture and art are other cultural traits that reflect the influence of religion. Islam and Arabic are found in the dome-shaped *mosques* with *minarets*, which also have geometric designs, *arabesque*, and *calligraphy*. Symbols of Judaism, including the Star of David, the *Menorah*, and the *Torah,* appear throughout Israel and the world, just as the cross or *crucifix* is displayed in the worship places of Christianity.

Clothing styles also reflect the importance of religions found in this region. Islamic women choose different ways to veil themselves according to sharia. Some Jewish and Christian believers also use headdresses to celebrate their beliefs in various fashions.

Dietary habits are influenced or dictated by religion. Many Jewish followers eat only *kosher* foods and often do not eat any pork products. Pork and alcohol are not allowed under Muslim law. It is quite evident that religion and culture impact this region in many different ways.

Humans spread culture in many ways. Traders and explorers, conquerors and armies, missionaries and travelers shared their beliefs and traditions worldwide. It is simple to identify the culture of a region by recognizing its human characteristics.

Name ______________________________

Identify which North Africa/Middle East religion is described by each characteristic:

J = Judaism C = Christianity I = Islam

Circle your choice. There may be more than one religion circled.

J C I	1. sharia	
J C I	2. monotheistic	
J C I	3. oldest	
J C I	4. youngest	
J C I	5. mosque	
J C I	6. cross	
J C I	7. Star of David	
J C I	8. veiled women	
J C I	9. kosher foods	
J C I	10. Jerusalem	

Each nation's type of government is given. Choose one of the nations listed below, research its government, summarize your findings, and present them to the class.

Afghanistan: transitional
Algeria: republic
Bahrain: traditional monarchy
Cyprus: republic
Egypt: republic
Iran: Islamic (theocratic) republic
Iraq: republic
Israel: republic
Jordan: constitutional monarchy
Kuwait: constitutional monarchy
Lebanon: republic
Libya: mass state (Jamahiriya = Islamic Arabic Socialist "Mass-State")
Morocco: constitutional monarchy
Oman: absolute monarchy
Qatar: traditional monarchy
Saudi Arabia: monarchy
Syria: republic (under military regime)
Tunisia: republic
Turkey: republic
United Arab Emirates: federation of emirates
Yemen: republic

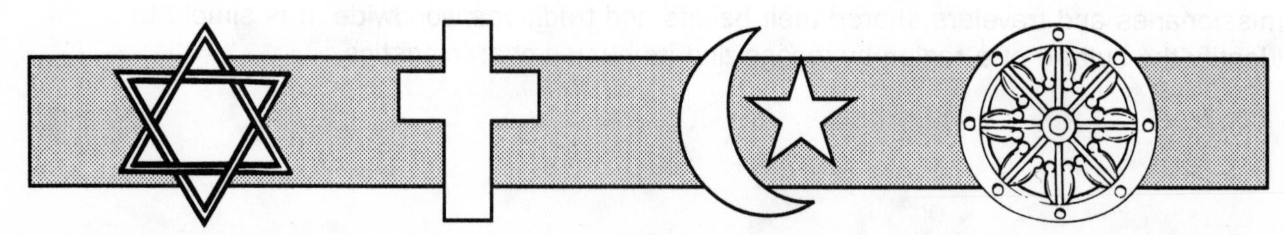

How Does Interaction Affect North Africa/Middle East?

Themes of Geography: *Location, Place, Interaction, Movement, Region*

Objectives

Students will

1. identify interdependence of petroleum and transportation
2. record historical data on a time line and make mathematical calculations related to the Suez Canal and OPEC
3. investigate environmental effects of dams
4. give a speech

Rationale

The presence of the Suez Canal and plentiful reserves of petroleum are features of this region that greatly affect the rest of the world. Over a century of history has been tied to this canal. The demand for petroleum in the last 60 years has increased the importance of the North Africa/Middle East region (especially the nations surrounding the Persian Gulf, which have two thirds of the world's known oil reserves). The financial security provided by the canal and the oil helps ensure economic stability for North Africa/Middle East countries.

Another environmental impact on this region comes from the dams which have been constructed. Economic, physical, and political relationships evolve as the structures are erected. Nowhere is this more evident than in Egypt and Turkey.

Skills Taught in This Unit

Map reading	Analysis	Computation
Relative location	Developing time line	Decimals (subtraction and division)
	Developing oral speech	Whole numbers (multiplication)

Vocabulary

Suez Canal	*Ferdinand de Lesseps*	*interdependence*	*Napoleon*
Aramco	*combustible*	*nationalized*	*OPEC*
emergency force	*embargo*	*quota*	*coalition*
annex	*tanker*	*pipeline*	*reserves*
hydroelectricity	*irrigation*	*reservoir*	*cataract*
upstream	*silt*	*mouth*	*delta*
erosion	*salinization*	*dam*	*Aswan*
Lake Nasser	*Ramses*	*Abu Simbel*	*Ataturk*
Anatolia	*Lake Assad*	*Persian Gulf War*	

Oil and Water in North Africa/Middle East

The twentieth century has brought recognition to the North Africa/Middle East region because so many countries have become so dependent on the petroleum found there. This need for oil has left the world so reliant on North Africa/Middle East that no one can deny the significance of this region's influence on the rest of the world.

Movement of people, goods, and services through the world's canals shows us the shortcuts we have developed, especially during times of unrest. The traditional antagonism among this region's states prevents North Africa/Middle East from possibly being one of the most powerful areas on the earth.

Materials: "Oil and Water in North Africa/Middle East" activity sheets, pencils, (optional: calculator)

Directions
Guide students' reading of the information on the activity sheets. Students record dates and events on the time line to summarize the article, use a map to identify the locations, and compute whole number and decimal calculations.

Dams in North Africa/Middle East

To consider the impact dams have on our environment is to study the history and future of North Africa/Middle East. When these barriers are constructed across nature's flowing waters, many environmental changes occur. Both negative and positive implications must be considered to understand the effects dams have on the world.

Materials: "Dams in North Africa/Middle East" activity sheets, pencils, (optional: atlases or other reference books)

Directions
Guide students' reading and answering of questions on the activity sheet. Simulate a conference setting with speaker's podium and microphone and students posing as the news media (reporters, camera crews, photographers), audience, and protesters.

Oil and Water in North Africa/Middle East

We often hear that water and oil do not mix. In North Africa/Middle East they mix as necessities for life and causes of conflict. Since the time *Ferdinand de Lesseps* completed the *Suez Canal* in 1869, the world has witnessed this *interdependence* of oil and water.

Napoleon ordered a survey in 1799, proposing a sea-level canal between the Mediterranean and Red Seas. This was abandoned and then revived in 1854, when de Lesseps acquired rights from Egypt to construct and operate a canal open to all nations' ships for 99 years. Thus, one of the world's leading trade routes, which shortens the distance from New York to India by 6000 kilometers, split Egypt and Africa from Asia. The steam yacht *Empress Eugenie* led the fleet opening the Suez Canal in 1869.

By 1908 the first Persian (now Iranian) oil field was discovered. Thirty years later, Saudi Arabia formed *Aramco*. Steam travel was being replaced with *combustible* engines. Iran's first oil field was *nationalized* in 1951.

In 1956 the Suez-Sinai War caused the canal to be nationalized, oil supplies to Europe to be cut off, and a United Nations *emergency force* to be established in Egypt to maintain peace. The next year, 1957, the Suez was closed to Israeli shipping for ten years, until 1967.

One influential alliance, the Organization of Petroleum Exporting Countries (*OPEC*), was created by Iran, Iraq, Kuwait, Saudi Arabia, and Venezuela in 1960. Originally, this was formed to oppose American and European oil price cuts. Qatar joined OPEC in 1961, Indonesia and Libya in 1962, and Abu Dhabi (part of the United Arab Emirates) in 1967.

The Six-Day War also occurred in 1967. During this Arab-Israeli war, an Arab oil *embargo* was begun, Iraq cut ties with the United States, and Egypt sunk ships in the Suez Canal. By 1969, Algeria had joined OPEC, and a revolution occurred in Libya.

The 1970s arrived and OPEC pressed for increased oil rates. Nigeria joined OPEC in 1971, and Ecuador and Gabon joined two years later. The year 1973 brought another Arab oil embargo against Europe, the United States, and Japan and the October Arab-Israeli War. Oil shortages were felt worldwide. Saudi Arabia became angry with the United States for supporting Israel during the war, but eventually a United Nations peacekeeping force was established in the Middle East. Oil prices stabilized from 1974-1978, when the Shah of Iran was overthrown and the Iranian oil crisis began. By 1979, OPEC was producing 66 percent of the world's petroleum, and the Egyptian-Israeli peace treaty allowed Israel to once again use the Suez Canal. Demand for oil dropped significantly worldwide.

Several tunnels for traffic were built under the Suez Canal in 1980. From 1980 until 1988, the Iran and Iraq War caused oil prices to triple. No Iraqi oil was shipped through the Persian Gulf.

During 1990, Iraq accused Kuwait and the United Arab Emirates of exceeding export *quotas* of oil. Iraq invaded Kuwait and *annexed* it as "province 19," leading to the *Persian Gulf War.* Thirty-one nations, in a *coalition* led by Saudi Arabia and the United States (largely financed by Saudi Arabia and Kuwait) came to Kuwait's defense. By February of 1991, the war against Iraq proved decisive in favor of the coalition forces. Iraq responded by dumping about 10 million barrels of oil into the Persian Gulf, causing one of the world's largest oil spills.

OPEC's world oil production was at 41 percent in 1992. Ecuador withdrew from OPEC in 1993, leaving Gabon, Indonesia, Iran, Nigeria, and Venezuela as non-Arab members. The Arab OPEC partners (Algeria, Iraq, Kuwait, Libya, Qatar, Saudi Arabia, and the United Arab

Name ____________________

Emirates) produce about one fourth of the world's oil. Much of this oil is transported in large *tankers* through the Suez Canal for two reasons. First, it can be sent to any port location at a lower cost than using *pipelines*. Second, when it is needed, the route of the oil shipment can be changed more quickly and easily than when it is being sent overland by pipeline.

There are 90 oil-producing nations in the world. Two thirds of the current known *reserves* are found in five Middle East nations which have immediate access to the Suez Canal. Oil and water can mix!

1. A time line gives a brief history of a topic. The article you just read about oil and water can be summarized in the time line below. Dates go on the left side of the line and the events on the right. Fill in the blanks.

Date	Event
1869	Suez Canal opened
____	Suez-Sinai War; Suez Canal nationalized
1960	____________________
____	Six-Day War; Egypt sank ships and closed Suez Canal
____	Arab-Israeli War; oil embargo against Europe, Japan, and United States
1979	OPEC produced ________ of world's oil
____	Iran-Iraq War; tripled oil prices
1982	Oil prices plummet.
____	OPEC maintaining shaky front.
1990	Persian Gulf War; Iraq invaded Kuwait
____	Iraq dumped oil into Persian Gulf

2. The Suez Canal extends from Port Said on the Mediterranean Sea to Port Tauflg near Suez on the Gulf of Suez that leads into the Red Sea. Draw the Suez Canal on this map. A symbol for a canal is: ┴┴┴┴

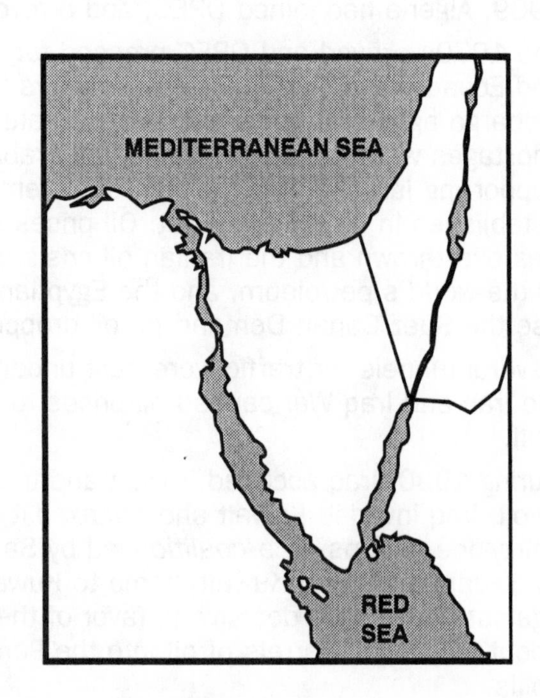

3. If oil is shipped from the port of Jibba on the west coast of Saudi Arabia to Europe, the tanker would travel through the __________ Sea, into the Gulf of Suez before entering the __________ to get into the Mediterranean Sea.
4. If the Middle East has approximately 70.4 percent of the world's proven oil reserves and Saudi Arabia has 25.9 percent of that amount, how much do Iraq, the United Arab Emirates, Kuwait, Iran, Libya, Egypt, Oman, Yemen, and Qatar have? ____________________
5. If 80 ships per day can travel through the Suez Canal, how many could possibly use this shortcut in a year? ____________________
6. If the average time to transit the Suez Canal is 15 hours and the canal's overall length is 193.5 kilometers, how many kilometers does a ship travel in one hour? __________

Dams in North Africa/Middle East

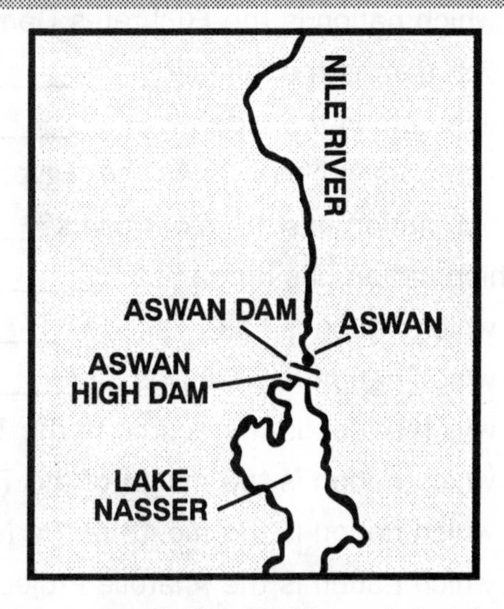

Dams are usually built to provide *hydroelectricity*, to control river flooding, for *irrigation*, and to create *reservoirs*, which are often used for recreation. But there are also side effects when dams are constructed on rivers.

The *Aswan* Dam was completed in 1902 at the first *cataract*, or rapids, 3½ miles up the Nile River from Aswan, Egypt. It was expanded three times until it reached its height of 175 feet in 1960. Then, with Soviet help, four miles farther *upstream* from the Aswan Dam, Egypt constructed the Aswan High Dam. It was finished in 1970 with a height of 375 feet. Not only was the High Dam taller than the original Aswan Dam, but it also tamed the annual flooding of the Nile, provided a year-round water supply for irrigation in Egypt and Sudan, increased the hydroelectric capacity for Egypt, and developed *Lake Nasser* as the largest freshwater lake in both Egypt and Sudan. It is the world's tenth largest rock-filled dam.

The dams created some negative environmental impact. Several historic landmarks from ancient Egypt (including the temple of *Ramses, Abu Simbel*) had to be moved away from the waters to preserve them. Many people in Sudan had to be resettled because their homes and farmland were under water. The amount of fertile *silt* below the dams has been greatly reduced, so expensive fertilizers have to be used by farmers. And since the silt is not being carried all the way to the *mouth* of the Nile River, the *delta* is not being naturally rebuilt. Coastal *erosion* on the Mediterranean Sea's shoreline is evident. Eastern Mediterranean sardine fisheries have ceased operation because of the silt decrease. *Salinization* in irrigated areas and saltiness in the Nile's waters have both increased. Lake Nasser is also collecting sediments more quickly than had been predicted. With droughts in Sudan to the south of this lake, its water level is dropping dramatically. Some are fearful of water and energy shortages in the future.

Another major dam project is found in Turkey. The world's ninth largest rock-filled dam, the *Ataturk*, was completed in 1993 at a height of 560 feet. When the *Anatolia* Project is completed, it will be one of 22 dams and 19 hydroelectric power stations on the Euphrates and Tigris Rivers in Turkey. The advantages for Turkey are the electricity these will produce plus the millions of acres of land they will help irrigate.

Syria's Euphrates Dam created *Lake Assad*, bringing hydroelectric power to Syria. The dam also doubled Syria's irrigated farmland. However, the resulting effects on the downstream country of Iraq have not been beneficial. The Euphrates Dam and Anatolia Project in Turkey divert vast amounts of water from the two rivers before they flow through Iraq. Iraq has no dams on either river to collect water for its use, and during the *Persian Gulf War*, the country's water supply was contaminated. Iraq is, therefore, dependent upon Turkey and Syria for the volume of water flowing through the Tigris and Euphrates Rivers.

Name ___________________________

1. In which nation is the Aswan High Dam? ___________________________
2. In which nation is the Ataturk Dam? ___________________________
3. In which nation is the Euphrates Dam? ___________________________
4. Which dam is the tallest? ___________________________
5. Which dam is the oldest? ___________________________
6. Which dam is closer to Aswan, Egypt? ___________________________
7. Which nation has the most dams? ___________________________
8. Which nation has no dams? ___________________________
9. In which nation is Lake Assad? ___________________________
10. In which nation is Lake Nasser? ___________________________
11. In which nation is the source of the Tigris-Euphrates Rivers? ___________________________
12. In which nation is the mouth of the Tigris-Euphrates Rivers? ___________________________
13. In which nation is the mouth of the Nile River? ___________________________
14. In which nation is the Anatolia Project? ___________________________

Conference Activity

An environmental conference is being held to discuss the following interactions between humans and their surroundings. You are the keynote speaker and must decide which of the following items you will mention as having positive or negative effects.

Circle your choice: + = positive - = negative

+	-	1. irrigation possibilities	+	-	5. flooded landmarks
+	-	2. flood control	+	-	6. people relocated
+	-	3. salinization	+	-	7. reservoirs created
+	-	4. ruined fisheries	+	-	8. hydroelectricity

What Are the North Africa/Middle East Regions?

Themes of Geography: *Location, Place, Region*

Objectives

Students will

1. identify and locate regions within North Africa/Middle East
2. evaluate regional hybridization

Rationale

The study of North Africa/Middle East regions shows important examples of regional interrelation in the world. These regions' influence upon each others' cultures, economic and political development, international relations, and use of resources are documented throughout history. There are many definitions and explanations for what constitutes the Middle East and North Africa, but the most important concept is the land connection between Asia, Europe, and Africa. That simple land link has shaped the past, present, and future of North Africa/Middle East.

Skills Taught in This Unit

Map reading
- Relative location
- Use of color key/legend

Vocabulary

subregion
peripheral
Maghreb

Regions Within North Africa/Middle East

In some studies of the world, North Africa is part of the African continent and the Middle East/Southwest Asia is part of the Asian continent. Within North Africa and the Middle East we find the following regions:

Egypt and the Lower Nile Basin: Egypt and northeastern Sudan
Maghreb: Morocco, Western Sahara, Algeria, Libya, and Tunisia
Non-Arab North: Turkey, Cyprus, Iran, and Afghanistan
Arabian Peninsula: Saudi Arabia, Yemen, Oman, the United Arab Emirates, Qatar, Bahrain, and Kuwait
Middle East: Iraq, Syria, Lebanon, Jordan, and Israel.

Also, the African Transition Zone is sometimes included as a *peripheral* of North Africa. When this is included, the nations of Mauritania, Mali, Niger, Chad, Sudan, Ethiopia, Eritrea, Djibouti, and Somalia are considered. For this unit's study, they are not considered as part of North Africa. Therefore, only the five regions mentioned above are usually considered as being North Africa and the Middle East/Southwest Asia.

Some geographers include Afghanistan as a part of South Asia. Western Sahara is not officially recognized by many, including major world organizations such as the United Nations and the World Bank.

Materials: "Regions Within North Africa/Middle East" activity sheet, colored pencils (markers or crayons), atlas (or other reference materials)

Directions
Carefully guide students' reading of the activity sheet. Note the differences of opinion on what is included in this region. Define *regional hybridization* and discuss why it occurs here. Refer to the nicknames given to this region in the previous activity "Relative Location of North Africa/Middle East."

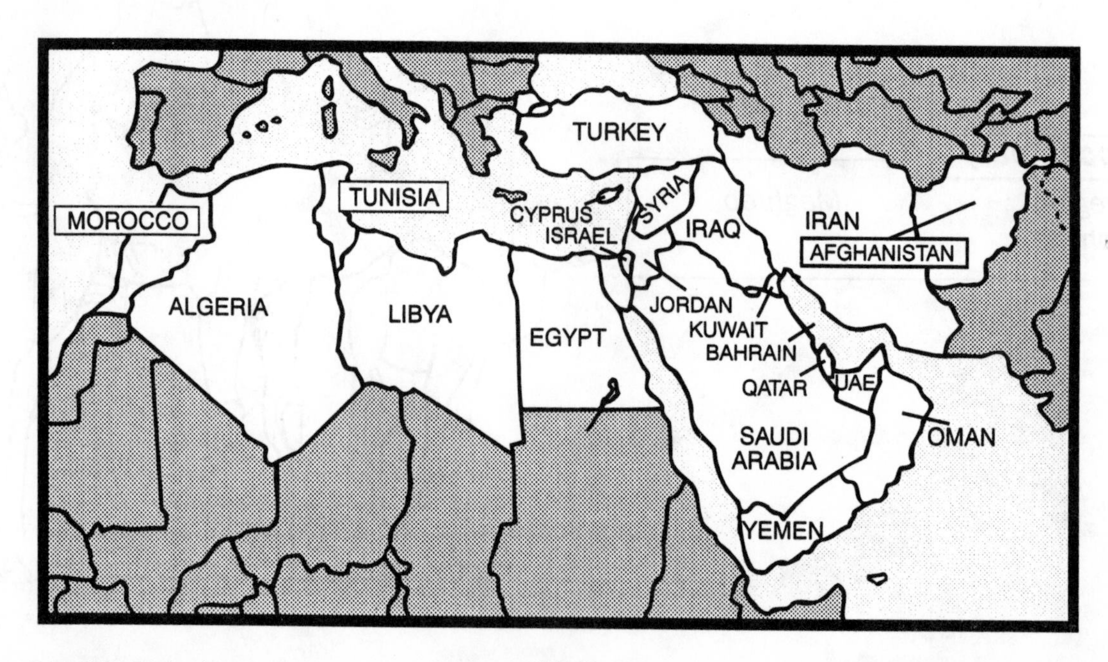

Name ______________________________

Regions Within North Africa/Middle East

The North Africa/Middle East region is generally divided into these five geographical *regions*: Egypt and the Lower Nile Basin, the Maghreb and its neighbors, the Non-Arab North, the Arabian Peninsula, and the Middle East. As countries are placed within these subregions, it will become clearer why this region is a connecting unit between Africa and Asia.

The Lower Nile Basin places northeastern Sudan and Egypt into their own subregion. *Maghreb* means "western isle" and includes Morocco, some of the disputed area of Western Sahara, most of Algeria and Libya, and Tunisia. Turkey, Cyprus, Iran, and Afghanistan compose the Non-Arab North. The Arabian Peninsula includes Saudi Arabia, Yemen, Oman, the United Arab Emirates, Qatar, Bahrain, and Kuwait. That leaves Iraq, Syria, Lebanon, Jordan, and Israel in the Middle East subregion. Confused? So are many others who now begin to see the overlap among nations, subregions, regions, cultures, and the world.

To "regionalize" the 22 countries on the map on the following page, color Maghreb, green; Egypt, orange; Middle East, red; Non-Arab North, yellow; and the Arabian Peninsula, brown.

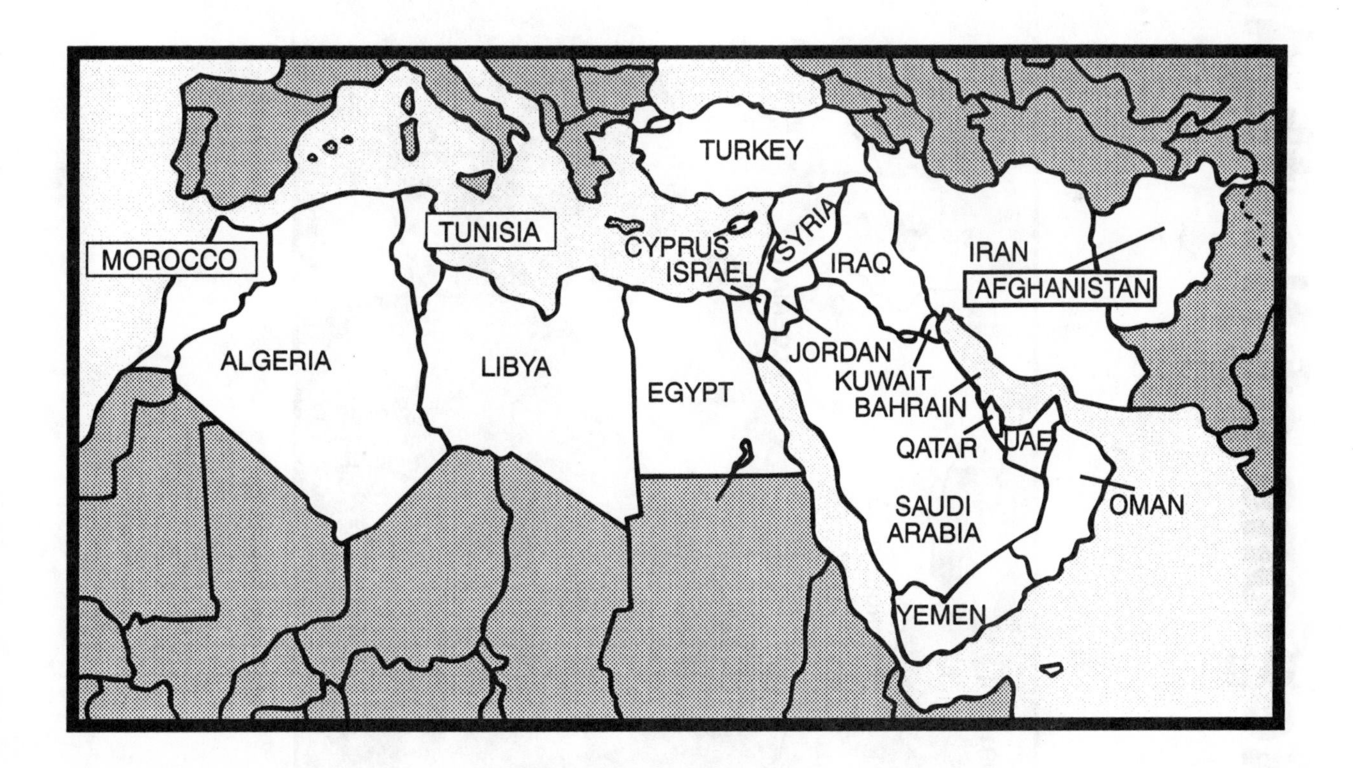

Regions of North Africa/Middle East

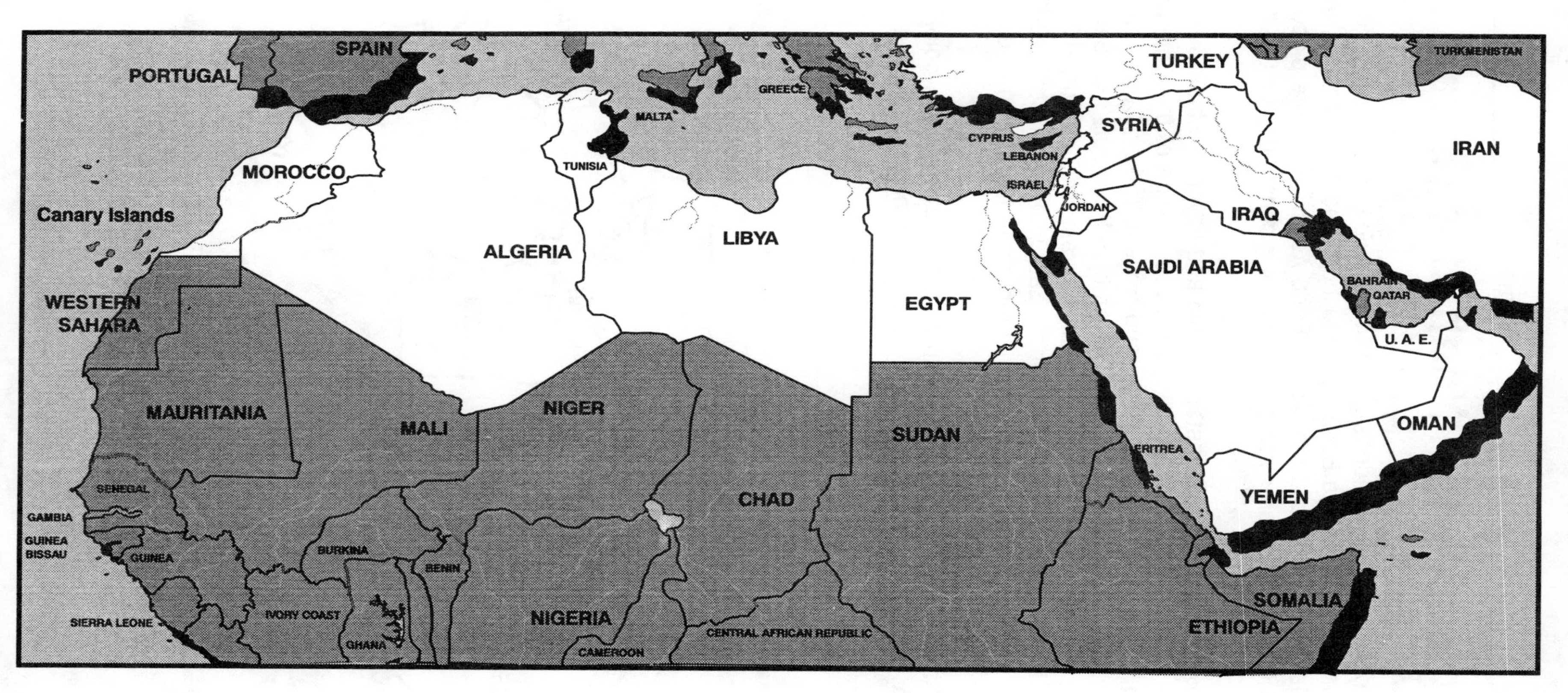

Asia

Where Is Asia?

Themes of Geography: *Location, Place, Region*

Objectives

Students will

1. use atlases and maps to identify absolute locations of Asian points of interest
2. analyze and identify relative locations of Asian land and water features
3. compose descriptions of relative locations in Asia

Rationale

Asia is the largest continent and is in many ways the most unique. It includes places or parts of countries and areas also included with Africa, Europe, Russia, and the Pacific world. This region encompasses almost every climate, biome, and soil, as well as every economic and political condition known to man.

There are several special land and water features found throughout Asia. Some are unique in size, others in color, and still others in age.

Skills Taught in This Unit

Map reading
- Absolute location
- Relative location

Analysis

Composition
- Descriptive writing

Vocabulary

Mt. Everest	*Caspian*	*subcontinent*	*archipelago*	*fossil fuel*
bauxite	*tungsten*	*manganese*	*nonrenewable*	*uranium*
Tonle Sap	*monsoon*	*sari*	*dhoti*	*Khyber Pass*
tundra	*kimchi*	*Suez Canal*	*Franz Josef*	*Dead Sea*
depression	*Andaman*	*Nicobar*	*channel*	*algae*
Huang	*loess*	*Gobi*	*estuary*	*Himalaya*

Absolute Location in Asia

From the days of Marco Polo to the present, the world has been fascinated by Asia. The images of wind-swept steppes, galloping Mongol hordes, wandering Bedouins, Arabian nights, and the mysteries of the Orient have enriched literature and cultures around the world. This lesson allows students to travel through Asia with their imaginations, and will meet the needs of all students' learning styles. Mental mapping is a vital technique for mastering location.

Materials: "Absolute Location in Asia" activity sheets, pencils, atlases and related reference books and materials, a large wall map of Asia, and a large wall map of the world. Optional materials: travel brochures, slides of Asian locations, old copies of *National Geographic* and travel magazines, Asian music (check library), colored pencils, magic markers, glue, construction paper, and other art supplies

Directions
Guide students' reading of the activity sheet. Ask several students using maps to help illustrate the areas contained in the reading. Then, assign a different region in Asia to each group of four to six students in the class. Structure group size to accommodate all the Asian regions. Instruct students to prepare a travelogue about their region. Suggest that the travelogue be both informative and interesting. Schedule class presentations by each group when the assignment is complete.

Relative Location in Asia

The unique range of Asia's geographical features is best characterized by the fact that within its area is the highest place on earth, Mt. Everest, and the lowest place on earth, the Dead Sea. Many other locations in Asia have widely contrasting geographical features.

Materials: "Relative Location in Asia" activity sheet cut into ten sections, pencils, a map of Asia taped or hung from a wall, atlases, encyclopedias and related reference books

Directions
Divide the class into ten groups. Give each group one of the ten activities. Groups will analyze and identify the location on their paper. Each student in the group must supply one hint to help the rest of the class guess the name of the location. As each location is guessed, a member of the winning group should identify the location on the map. Extend the activity by asking each group to make up a new puzzling location.

Absolute Location in Asia

Asia is the largest of all the continents. It covers nearly one third of the earth's land surface and is home to more than half of humankind. Most geographers identify 47 countries as being Asian.

Earth's highest mountains, the *Himalayas*, are located in Asia. *Mt. Everest* is the highest peak in the Himalayas and in the world. The lowest point below sea level on land, the *Dead Sea*, is also part of Asia. Europe and Asia share the *Caspian* Sea, a salt lake which is the largest inland body of water in the world. Asia is the only continent with a *subcontinent*, India. Volcanic islands of Southeast Asia are *archipelagoes*; Indonesia and the Philippines are both archipelagoes.

Asia has vast natural resources. *Fossil fuels, nonrenewable* water resources, and human resources are a few of them. Mineral resources, many untapped so far, are powerful assets that will carry this region into the future. Tin, coal, iron, *manganese, tungsten,* as well as reserves of nickel, *bauxite*, copper, and *uranium*, give Asia a varied resource base. Southeast Asia's large reserves of petroleum, particularly in Brunei and Malaysia, are also important.

Some of the world's greatest rivers are located in Asia. The Indus, Ganges, and Brahmaputra of southern Asia, the east Asian Huang He (Yellow), Chang Jiang (Yangzi), and Xi Jang (West) Rivers are joined by the Mekong flowing into Southeast Asia with the Irrawaddy, Salween, Chao Phraya, and Red rivers.

Metropolitan areas are responsible for Asia's three-billion-plus population centers—Tokyo, Japan; Shanghai, China; Bombay, India; Beijing, China; Calcutta, India; and Seoul, South Korea. These are six of the ten most populated cities in the world. Major ports such as Singapore, Hong Kong, and Yokohama, Japan, are significant also.

Name ______________________________

With the vastness of Asia, we can best see this location from above the earth. Let's take a trip by air to pinpoint many of these places you have read about. We will begin in Southeast Asia and travel clockwise around this region. Get your passport, an atlas, and we're off from western North America . . . to Java (most densely populated area of the world) in Indonesia at 1.______°S ______°E, on to Singapore at 2.______°N ______°E for some shopping at Lucky Plaza, then to 3.______°N ______°E to visit in the capital, Bandar Seri Begawan, built on stilts in one of the world's wealthiest nations.

Leaving Brunei, we go over former French Indochina and the Mekong River to Cambodia (or Kampuchea) and their *Tonle Sap* at 4.______°N ______°E, which can quadruple in size during the monsoon season.

Monsoons also affect Bangladesh, so we're off to Dhaka on the delta of the Ganges-Brahmaputra Rivers at 5.______°N ______°E to visit houses on mud platforms.

Our next lofty destination is high in the Himalayas of Nepal (on the border with China)—Mt. Everest at 6.______°N ______°E—we're on top of the world at 29,864 feet. Next we come back down to earth with millions of people in Bombay, India, at 7.______°N ______ E, purchasing some textiles, maybe a colorful *sari* or a homespun *dhoti.*

Next we'll slip over the *Khyber Pass,* as invaders often did heading into Southwest Asia at 8.______°N ______°E, before making our way to 9.______°N ______°E and the Sinai Peninsula, also seeing the *Suez Canal.*

From this northeast corner of Egypt we travel to the Dead Sea at 10.______°N ______°E to prove we can truly float in this salty water; then it's on to Istanbul, Turkey—also known historically as Constantinople—(the only city in the world on two continents) at 11.______°N ______°E.

The next leg of this journey finds us passing over the boundary line many mapmakers use to divide Asia from Europe with the Caspian Sea at 12.______°N ______°E, and into the treeless *tundra* of Russia's Arctic north to *Franz Josef* land above the Arctic Circle—and Asia's northern edge—at 13.______°N ______°E—brrrrrrrr, cold!

Flying in a great circle route southeast to 14.______°N ______°E, we arrive in the world's largest city, Tokyo, Japan . . . how about some Disney fun while we're here before we head to 15.______°N ______°E for some *kimchi* in Seoul, South Korea?

Manchuria's (or as the Chinese prefer "Northeast") coal and oil fields can be seen at 16.______°N ______°E around Harbin as we fly over, going southwest past the Great Wall of China to see the capital, Beijing, at 17.______°N ______°E, then further along China's Grand Canal route to 18.______°N ______°E and Shanghai, the world's largest city.

We finish our Asian travels in Hong Kong at 19.______°N ______°E, fascinated by the modern skyscrapers.

Create a paragraph about your personal impressions of your trip.

Name ______________________________

Relative Location in Asia

For this assignment, you are to become a geographical specialist to identify these Asian locations. Use your analytical abilities and any reference material you need to reveal the identity of each of these Asian features. Some are real world champions!

1. I am the largest saltwater lake in the world. I am surrounded by five nations, and my surface is 92 feet below sea level. I have a *depression* on my northern shoreline, and it is no wonder my mental state leaves me with an identity crisis, because everyone calls me a sea—I'm so depressed! ________
2. I am the world's largest sea. My name is tied to Southeast and East Asia, but cousin East has his own identity . . . don't ask me what happened to cousins North and West. I create a split personality for Malaysia. ______________
3. I get two claims to fame! I am the lowest point on land and the lowest lake in the world. My surface water is 1,302 feet below sea level to be exact. I am so salty that I am uninhabitable and much saltier than the oceans. Wow! ______________
4. I am the largest peninsula in the world. My shape like a snow boot is really misleading because my dry climate would not produce that kind of precipitation. My identity is shared with others in this region, a country, a culture, and a language. Sharing is wonderful!________
5. I am the oldest and deepest lake in the world, but I still do not get the respect I deserve. Children slide on my icy surface in the parts that remain frozen for up to seven months of the year. ____________
6. I am the largest bay in the world. The *Andaman* and *Nicobar* islands are located in me. Between the maze of *channels* across the world's largest delta from the Ganges-Brahmaputra rivers dumping water into me and my high tides during the summer monsoon, I feel like I barely keep my head above water! ____________________________
7. I am the largest archipelago in the world. My 13,677 islands string together under the motto "unity in diversity." With some 300 ethnic groups speaking more than 250 languages, we crowd onto just a few of these many islands. ____________
8. I am the color my name implies because *algae* live in my sea water. The sands of Egyptian and Arabian deserts also irritate my eyes, making them this color.

   ____
9. I am a Chinese river that they call *Huang*. My "color" name comes from the tons of soil called *loess* I carry from the great *Gobi* Desert of interior Asia into a sea. This must be my sibling called by the same color-name. You might as well identify us both! _________
10. I am Asia's longest *estuary*, and I am also one of the few rivers that flows into the Arctic Ocean. Does that make me a twin? Not necessarily, if you know what an estuary is. Mine is 550 miles long and as wide as 50 miles. ____________

How Is Asia Unique?

Themes of Geography: *Location, Place, Region*

Objectives

Students will
1. examine earth's surface (geomorphology)
2. graph and investigate population

Rationale

Geomorphology is the study of the configuration of the earth's solid surface, encompassing landscapes and landforms. These physical features are slowly but constantly changing. Water, wind, and ice cause most of these changes in the earth's crust. Our earth's restlessness invites a scientific study of Asia's physical geography in the lithosphere and hydrosphere.

There are many people in Asia. If the people of China stood on one another's shoulders, they could make three chains stretching from the earth to the moon. Imagine how many chains could be made with all of Asia's 3,247,000,000 people (China's population is 1,203,097,288)! Asia has the largest population and some of the most crowded areas in the world.

Skills Taught in This Unit

Map reading
Relative location
Graphing
Population pyramid
Analysis

Vocabulary

tectonic · *erosion* · *weathering* · *plates* · *trench*
rift valley · *Ring of Fire* · *volcano* · *earthquake* · *landslide*
seismic · *tsunami* · *waterfall* · *subcontinent* · *climate*
silt · *loess* · *sandbar* · *delta* · *typhoon*
cyclone · *monsoon* · *glacier* · *fjord* · *desert*
population · *birth rate* · *death rate* · *population increase* · *Pangaea*
infant mortality · *life expectancy* · *population density* · *population pyramid*
axis · *distribution* · *rapid growth* · *slow growth*
negative growth · *no growth* · *census* · *aquaculture*

Physical Place Characteristics in Asia

According to one theory, earth's continents once were all one supercontinent called *Pangaea*. About 200 million years ago, Pangaea began pulling apart. According to the theory of plate tectonics, the continents rode on crustal plates pushed by the flow of partly molten rock in the earth's upper mantle.

The southern continents formed Gondwana in the southern part of Pangaea. Africa was at the heart of Gondwana, with North and South America, Antarctica, Australia, and India radiating out from this core. The breakup of Pangaea was only the most recent in a series of continental separations and collisions that have occurred in the earth's history.

Materials: continental map cut into continent puzzle pieces, "Physical Place Characteristics in Asia" activity sheets, pencil

Directions
Brainstorm with students to find what creates the physical features of the earth. Guide students' discussion toward continental drift with plate tectonics. Use the continent puzzle pieces to display how the present-day continents could have formed Pangaea and Gondwana. Lead students' reading of the activity sheet.

Human Place Characteristics in Asia

Population and population density offer the ultimate study in human characteristics of a location. Using population pyramids which give population data by gender and age, growth rates (and distribution) can be analyzed as zero, slow, rapid, and negative growth.

Birth rate, death rate, population increase, life expectancy, and infant mortality are all included in the analysis of population. Doubling rates and exponential growth can be juxtaposed with this analysis. Asia has the world's largest populations. This region offers the best chance to understand the demands humans impose on a place.

Materials: "Human Place Characteristics in Asia" activity sheets, pencil, ten chairs, at least eight students (or as many as 12 to 16)

Directions
Guide students' reading of the activity sheets. As study partners, have students compare their Japanese population pyramids. After reviewing the written portion of the activity sheets, place ten chairs together in a space representing Japan's land area. Have eight students sit on the ten chairs to illustrate Japan's population density. To show China's population density, have four more students sit on the ten chairs. Adding 16 more students will demonstrate Taiwan's population density. If Hong Kong's population density could be shown, 140 additional students would have to be invited to sit on the ten chairs.

Physical Place Characteristics in Asia

There are several forces that formed the Asia we know. *Tectonic, erosion,* and *weathering* forces have affected the land and are still changing this vast region.

Tectonic means "builder." Earth's seven huge and other smaller thick, rock *plates* are always moving slowly around the globe. Forces inside our planet cause this movement. When the plates collide, tall mountain chains, such as Asia's Himalayas, or high plateaus, such as Tibet's, are formed. Many say the Indian-Australian Plate is moving the *subcontinent* of India further into the Eurasian Plate, another example of tectonics. A *trench* may be formed when one plate slides beneath another, such as the *rift valley* of Southwest Asia. The *Ring of Fire* is a zone around the Pacific plate which consists of hundreds of active *volcanoes.* Twenty percent of the world's volcanoes are in Indonesia. Japan's Mt. Fuji is also located in the Ring of Fire.

An *earthquake* occurs when plates build up tension as they slide alongside each other and catch. The 1995 earthquake in western Japan devastated the city of Kobe and surrounding areas. Earthquakes, *landslides,* and volcanism can also cause *seismic* sea waves called *tsunami* or *waterfalls.*

While forces from the interior of the earth affect the earth, the surface of the earth experiences weathering and erosion. Repeated temperature changes and chemical action in the wet atmosphere result in climate changes. Asia has every type of climate somewhere across its vast area. *Climate* is the main cause of the crumbling of the earth's surface rocks. Erosion occurs when weathered rock is changed and destroyed by glaciers, rivers, waves, and winds. For example, eroded rocks such as China's Loess Plateau resulted in fertile *silt (loess)* being carried by the Huang River to the Yellow Sea. The silt gives both rivers their yellow tint. Other erosion changes were caused by building up the earth's rocks, as seen in *sandbars* at the *delta* (mouth) of the Ganges-Brahmaputra Rivers. Water erosion occurs with *typhoons* and *cyclones* striking land in the Indian and Pacific Oceans. Erosion is common when *monsoons* bring rain to South and Southeast Asia. Running water is the most effective and widespread of all erosion agents. Many valleys are carved through mountains by rivers that extend their deltas into the seas.

Ice erosion is mostly caused by *glaciers.* The *fjords* of Japan were carved by glaciers eating away at the coastline. These ice sheets also went into mountain valleys thousands of years ago widening and deepening river valleys.

Wind causes the greatest problems in dry locations. Most of the world's *deserts* are not sandy, but have rocky landscapes. Some thick sand deposits blown about by wind have formed dunes in Asia as in the Arabian desert.

Humans also create changes in the Asian landscape. Land-use practices such as surface mining, agriculture and *aquaculture,* development of cities, and water diversions change the physical features of Asia.

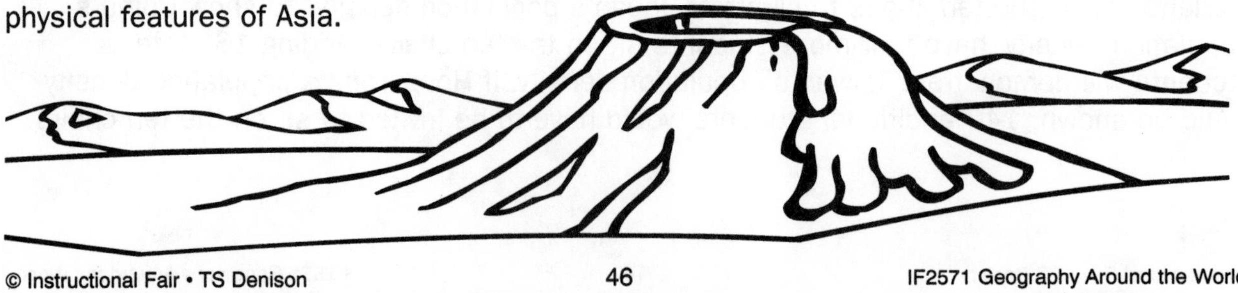

Name ______________________________

This graphic organizer will compare and contrast the two forces highlighted in your reading. Give two similarities of tectonics and erosion and weathering. Then, choose two situations in which tectonics and erosion/weathering have different effects. Use two examples for each situation.

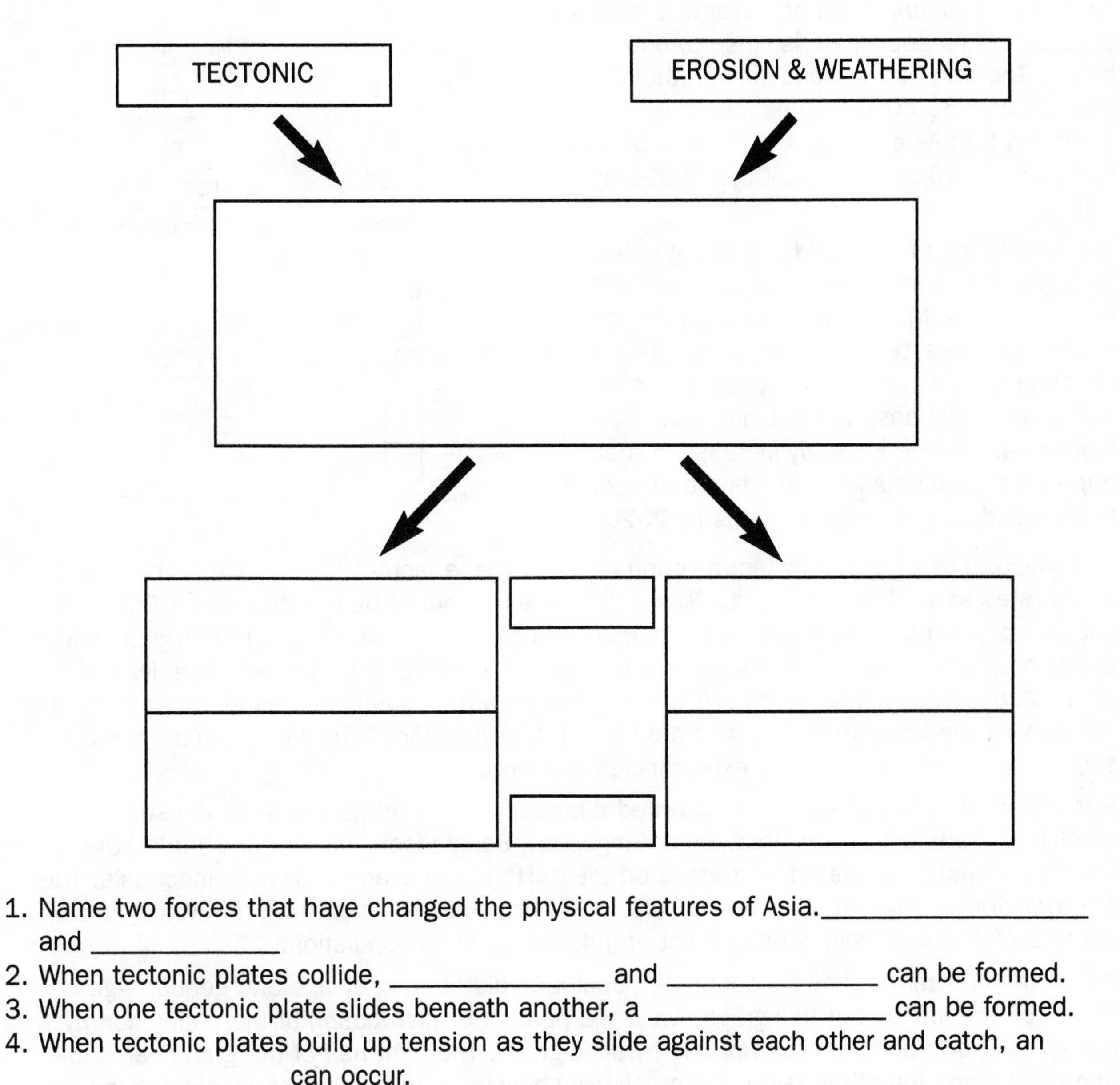

1. Name two forces that have changed the physical features of Asia. ________________ and ____________
2. When tectonic plates collide, ______________ and ______________ can be formed.
3. When one tectonic plate slides beneath another, a ______________ can be formed.
4. When tectonic plates build up tension as they slide against each other and catch, an ______________ can occur.
5. Name the main cause of the weathering of the earth's rock surfaces. ____________
6. ____________ is when weathered rock is removed from its source and carried away.
7. Name three kinds of erosion. ______________________

   ____

   ____

Name ____________________

Human Place Characteristics in Asia

Fourteen Asian nations have 55 percent of the world's *population.* China has over one billion people. India's population is close to one billion. The other 12 nations provide the balance of 3,500,000,000 people. It is projected that Asia will have close to 4 billion people by 2010 and over 4,300,000,000 by 2020.

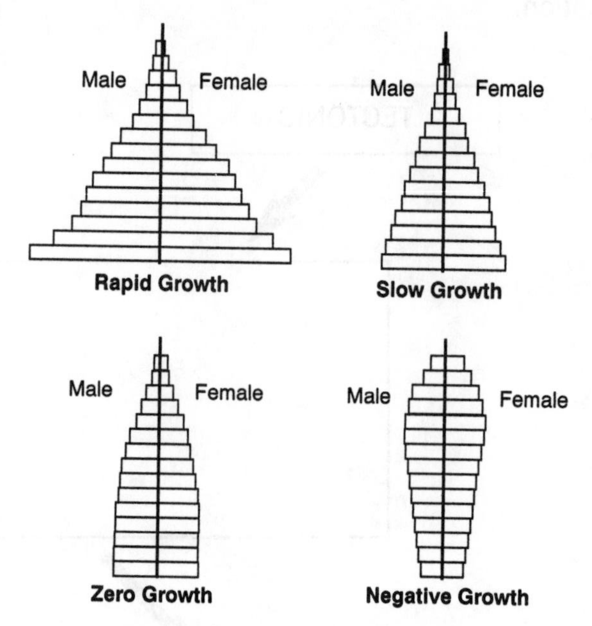

The population of the world is growing older. By 2025, there will be more people over 60 than under 25. Many Asian countries do not share this characteristic. Younger people will continue to dominate for many years to come. These Asian nations, China, India, and Indonesia, will see a steady increase in their populations. Some Asian nations are projected to almost double their populations by 2020.

Many factors determine how fast a country grows. These factors can include its birth and death rates as well as family size. *Birth rate* is the number of babies born per 1,000 in a nation's population. *Death rate* is the number of people who die per 1,000 in the population. By taking the birth rate of a country and subtracting its death rate, you will have its *population increase. Infant mortality* is also studied with population. This is the number of babies who die for every 1,000 who are born. *Life expectancy* is how long a citizen in a country can expect to live. Life expectancies are measured in years.

Population density measures how crowded a place is. The world's five most densely populated areas are Asian: Hong Kong, Singapore, Bangladesh, Taiwan, and Japan. One of the most densely populated land areas on the earth is the island of Java in Indonesia. There are over 500 people per square mile (over 193 per square kilometer) on this volcanic island the size of Alabama; this is 60 percent of Indonesia's total population.

A *population pyramid* shows a country's population distribution by age and gender. Age is shown on the left *axis* of this graph, while the percent of *distribution* of the population by gender is shown on the bottom of this pyramid-graph. The right half of the graph can show one gender and the other half of the graph will show the other gender. A pyramid graph that is straight and shapeless means the country is developed and rich. One that has a big bulge in the middle of the graph means the nation is becoming rich. An actual pyramid shape on the graph means the country is poor and developing at a much slower rate than the remainder of the world. These are sometimes called 1) *rapid growth,* 2) *slow growth,* 3) *negative growth,* and 4) *no growth* when compared from year to year as populations are counted in a *census.*

Name ______________________________

Using the population statistics below, fill in the graph. Shade the blocks. Each block represents 1 million people. Shade half of a block for half million people.

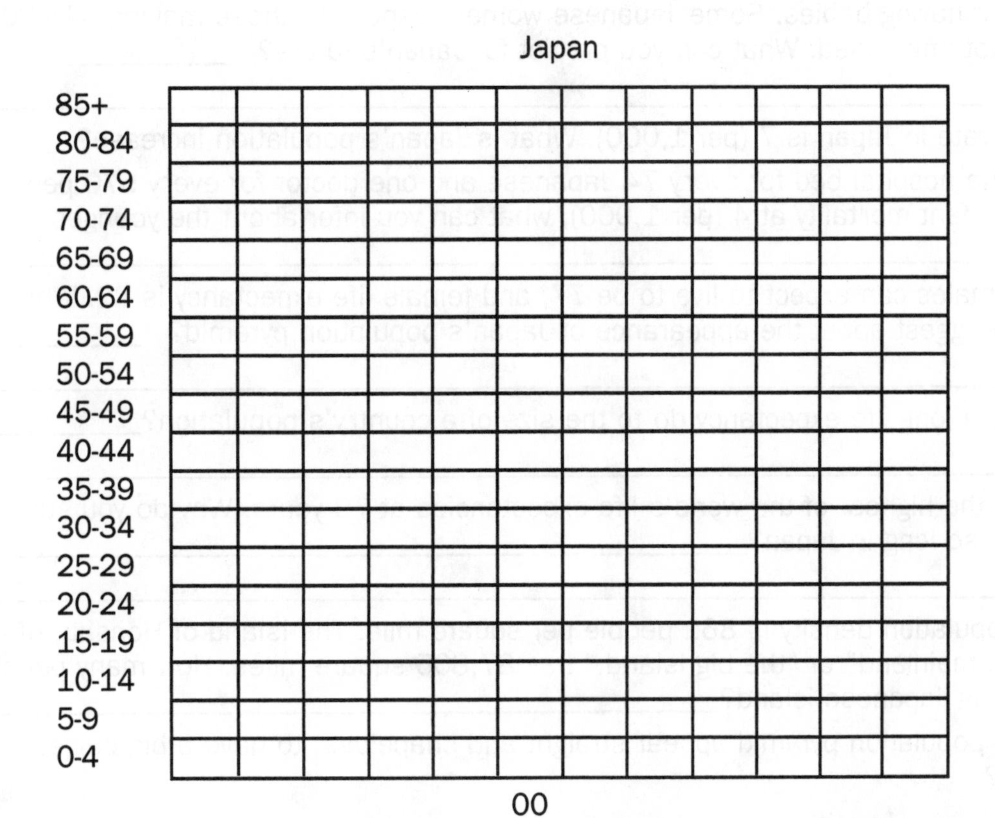

Ages	Males	Females
0-4	3,000,000	3,000,000
5-9	3,000,000	3,000,000
10-14	4,000,000	4,000,000
15-19	4,500,000	4,000,000
20-24	5,000,000	5,000,000
25-29	4,500,000	4,000,000
30-34	4,000,000	4,000,000
35-39	4,000,000	4,000,000
40-44	4,500,000	4,500,000
45-49	5,000,000	5,000,000
50-54	4,500,000	4,500,000
55-59	4,000,000	4,000,000
60-64	3,500,000	4,000,000
65-69	3,000,000	3,000,000
70-74	2,000,000	2,500,000
75-79	1,000,000	2,000,000
80+	1,000,000	2,000,000

Name ____________________

1. As of 1995, Japan's population was 125 million people; how many are in your age group? ____________________
2. Japan's birth rate is 11 (per 1,000). It is the lowest birth rate of any industrialized nation. Fearing a labor shortage in the future, the Japanese government has offered bonuses for having babies. Some Japanese women, especially those making $45,000 a year, are not impressed. What can you predict for Japan's future? ____________________
3. The death rate in Japan is 7 (per 1,000). What is Japan's population increase? ______
4. There is one hospital bed for every 74 Japanese and one doctor for every 570 people. With their infant mortality at 4 (per 1,000), what can you infer about the youngest Japanese? ____________________
5. Japanese males can expect to live to be 77, and female life expectancy is 82. What does this suggest about the appearance of Japan's population pyramid? ____________________
6. What does a long life expectancy do to the size of a country's population? ____________________
7. Japan has the highest of the world's life expectancies at 79 years. Why do you suppose people live so long in Japan? ____________________
8. Japan's population density is 861 people per square mile. The island of Honshu, often called "the mainland" or "the big island," has 87,805 square miles. How many people populate this Japanese island? ____________________
9. Is Japan's population pyramid appear straight and shapeless, to have a big bulge, or as a pyramid? ____________________
10. Which of the following best describes Japan's population? (Circle one in each line.)

a. lots of babies	average number of babies	fewer babies
b. lots and lots of workers	average number of workers	fewer workers
c. lots of seniors	average number of seniors	fewer seniors

11. Does Japan's population pyramid show it is developed or developing? ____________________
12. Is more of Japan's population under 15 years of age or over 65 years of age? ______
13. Natural increase of the population is .3 percent in Japan. It is 1.1 percent in China, 1.6 percent in Indonesia, and 1.8 percent in India. What does this tell you about these four Asian nations? ____________________
14. What occurred in Japan about 50 years ago that led to the shading on your pyramid for the age groups 50-59, varying from a pattern begun with the 45-49 age group? ______
15. Japan is one of 14 Asian countries that has 55 percent of the world's population. What can you predict for Japan's and Asia's future? ____________________

How Does Interaction Affect Asia?

Themes of Geography: *Location, Place, Interaction, Movement, Region*

Objectives

Students will
1. examine technology and its movement through time
2. construct a mental map
3. create a technological project
4. analyze agriculture and its economic effects
5. compose a clarification paragraph

Rationale

Movement of ideas and techniques can be seen in technology. Many consider Asia "developing," when actually it has been quite advanced and "developed" throughout time and history. At any given point in recorded history, Asian civilizations have excelled at providing humans with methods and inventions that are still in use today.

Economic geography studies livelihood patterns and the relative wealth of national groups on a global scale. Agriculture is humanity's leading occupation. From agriculture spring many other manufacturing and service occupations. Developing countries practice both ancient farming techniques and modern agronomy.

Technology and agricultural practices change the environment, while advances in technology and agriculture change world civilizations.

Skills Taught in This Unit

- Map reading
  - Relative location
- Analysis
- Composition
  - Clarification writing

Vocabulary

Han	*porcelain*	*seismograph*	*Ts'ai Lun*
Ming	*Qing*	*livestock*	*compass*
abacus	*woodblocks*	*Marco Polo*	*Meiji*
zero	*decimal*	*water clock*	*geometry*
algebra	*astronomy*	*pyramid*	*arch*
Fertile Crescent	*crop yield*	*Green Revolution*	*collective*
migratory	*plantation*	*subsistence*	*communist*
slash and burn	*commercial*	*arable*	
terrace	*monsoon*	*economic geography*	

Technology in Asia

Throughout Asian history, various cultures have invented and discovered numerous innovations still in use today. The movement and exchange of innovations have brought parts of the world closer together. Technology of the past is often taken for granted today, and today's discoveries will become passé tomorrow.

Materials: "Technology in Asia" activity sheet, pencil, paper, various supplies (art, computer)

Directions
Brainstorm the definition of *technology*. Guide students' reading of the activity sheet. Redefine *technology*. Also, define and discuss economic geography and how it relates to this activity and the next.

Agriculture in Asia

Agriculture has been a basic human practice since civilizations began. Economic geography cannot be studied without examining the basic types of farming practiced worldwide. Studying the interaction of agriculture and the environment gives us a fundamental understanding of people's relationship with their world.

Clarification writing should be distinguished from point-of-view writing. No opinion should be given in the clarification style. Substantiating facts to justify the writer's topic and main ideas is what is most important in clarification compositions.

Materials: green construction paper, "Agriculture in Asia" activity sheets, chalkboard or overhead projector w/acetate roller or transparency film, overhead pen or pencil, pencil, paper (computer)

Directions
While holding up green paper, ask students what this color symbolizes to them. Guide students' reading of the activity sheet, categorizing farming types on the chalkboard or overhead projector. Note the students who use a graphic organizer as prewriting for their paragraph and encourage those who do not to use this strategy.

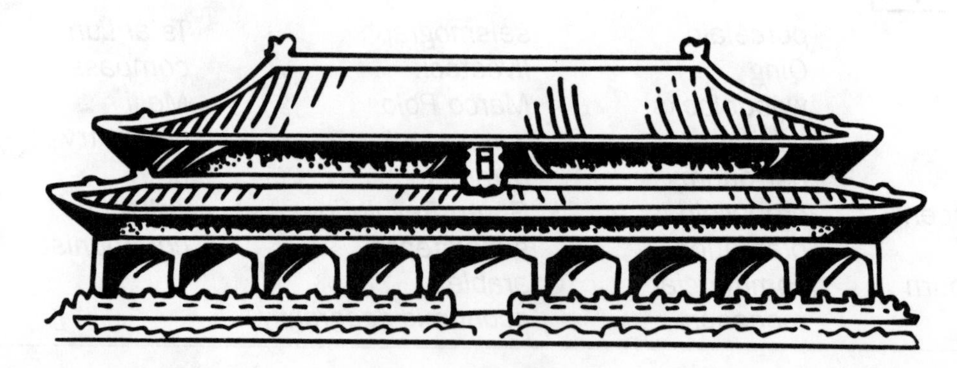

Name ______________________________

Technology in Asia

Early Asian civilizations improved life for people throughout time with the discoveries and inventions they contributed to the world. Many of these innovations are taken for granted today.

Dating back to 202 B.C., the Chinese *Han* dynasty gave the world three innovations—the first true paper, *porcelain*, and a primitive *seismograph*. In A.D. 105, *Ts'ai Lun* developed paper from rags, old fish netting, and tree bark. The Chinese kept this a secret for 500 years. Porcelain as a ceramic art form was joined by bronze, jade, and textiles (particularly silk) and later brought fame to two Chinese dynasties (*Ming, Qing*).

China is located in an area known for earthquakes. The seismograph, which measures and records earthquake vibrations, was created in China thousands of years ago.

China further established itself in the technological world through the travels of *Marco Polo* in 1275. After his travels throughout China, he returned to his native Italy with stories of printed money, gunpowder, the *compass*, the *abacus*, and silk and paper prints made with *woodblocks* and movable type. The innovations fascinated Europeans, who became eager to travel and trade with the "Orient." Trade introduced Asia's innovations to Europe and eventually to the rest of the world.

Japan is also a source of Asian technological advances. During the seventh century, the Japanese acquired the knowledge of making paper and began producing paper through mass production. During the *Meiji* era (1868-1912), Japan imported technology for industrial, commercial, and educational purposes. This industrial productivity led companies like SONY and other Japanese companies to become world leaders in technology. More recent inventions of this company are the video cassette and the compact disc player.

During the period from the fourth to the seventh centuries, India's Gupta dynasty invented the *zero* and *decimal* point, plastic surgery, and *water clock*. Indians also wove cotton and rust-proofed iron.

In Southwest Asia, the Arabs developed arithmetic, *geometry, algebra, astronomy*, writing systems, calendars, and engineering wonders (*pyramids* and the *arch*).

List below the 25 Asian discoveries and innovations mentioned in the reading.

Agriculture in Asia

Farming is an important way humans interact with the environment. The first agricultural efforts in history were in Southwest Asia's *Fertile Crescent*. About 750 years ago, an average-sized field of wheat might have provided enough food for five people for a year. Today, the same field in a developed country would feed between 20 and 50 people for a year and supply enough seed to sow for the next crop.

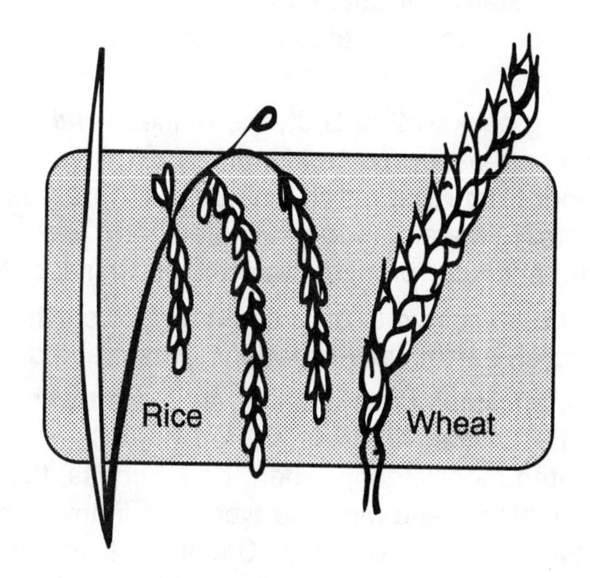

One reason such *crop yield* has increased is the "*Green Revolution*" of the 1960s. The gap between food production and world population has been narrowed with the development of high-yielding crop varieties, particularly rice and wheat. These new breeds respond well to fertilizers and irrigation. Rice from the Philippines is used in India, Malaysia, Pakistan, and Turkey. Japan and Taiwan have quadrupled their rice production, now that they have the financial ability to obtain fertilizers and irrigation. With world organizations training Asian scientists and technicians to make better use of new technologies, Asia has the potential to feed itself. Although some problems still exist, the transfer and diffusion of agricultural technology from technologically developed nations to less advanced agricultural areas are occurring and will continue.

There are four main types of agriculture practiced throughout Asia—*collective, migratory, plantation,* and *subsistence*. Collective agriculture is found mainly in government-controlled nations. There are fewer *communist*-controlled countries in Asia. Therefore, countries are starting to relax their agricultural controls. In a collective agricultural system, the government directs farmers to grow certain crops. Then, most of the crop is distributed by the government. Migratory agriculture is the oldest farming method. It is practiced mainly in Asia's rain forests. The *slash-and-burn* method, where trees are cut down and burned to clear for farming, is still used to plant rice, beans, cassava, corn, and yams. Plantation agriculture is the *commercial* style of farming. Usually one crop, such as coffee, palm oil, rubber, sugar, or tea, is grown for export. Some Asian nations depend on these commodities as real moneymakers in their economies. The fourth type, subsistence agriculture, is the most widely practiced of all types of Asian farming. Farmers produce enough to feed their families but have nothing left to sell. *Arable* farmers (growing crops) and *livestock* farmers (keeping animals) are often subsistence farmers. They survive on small farms (averaging about six acres), do not own their own land (may be in debt to landowner), and farm in coastal lowlands, in river plains, or on *terraced* hillsides that are affected by *monsoons*.

Farmers try to produce as much as they can from their land. To do this, they adapt to and improve the natural environment so they can get a bigger harvest.

Name ____________________

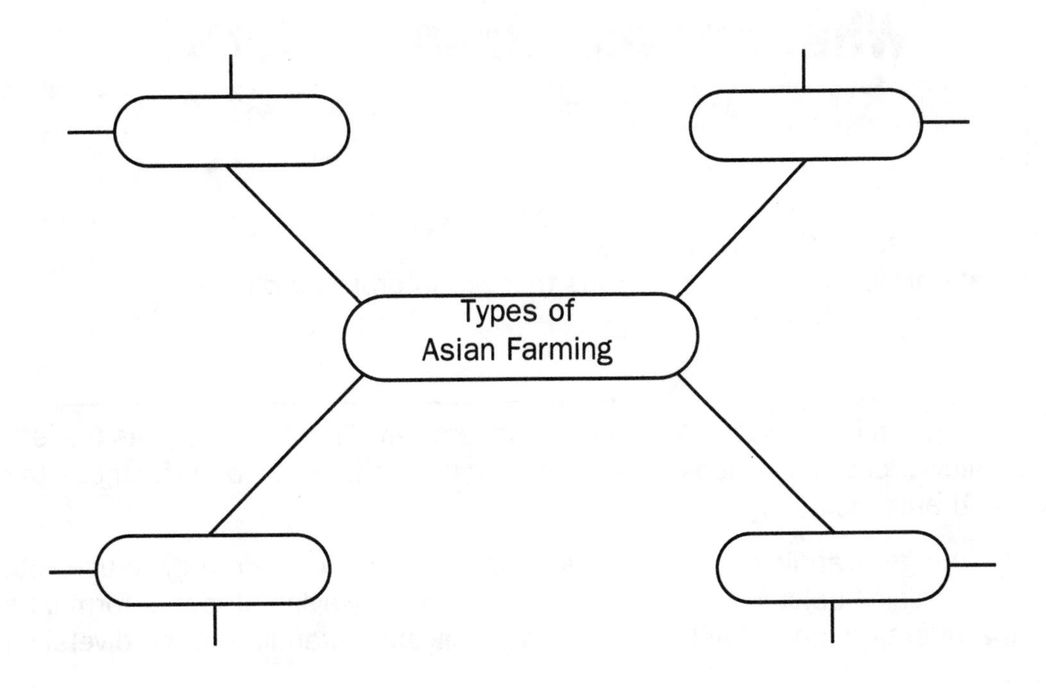

Produce a graphic organizer summarizing the types of farming found in Asia. Give two facts about each type.

1. Where in Asia was farming first practiced? ____________________
2. What occurred during the 1960s that led to improved agricultural techniques in developing nations? ____________________
3. Which crops had high-yield varieties developed during the Green Revolution? ____________________
4. List seven Asian nations using high-yield variety rice. ____________________
5. How does slash-and-burn agriculture affect the environment? ____________________

On a separate sheet, compose a clarification paragraph on why you feel agriculture is tied to *economic geography*.

What Are the Asian Regions?

Themes of Geography: *Location, Place, Region*

Objectives

Students will
1. identify and locate regions within Asia
2. differentiate places within Asian regions that are interpreted differently

Rationale

Although it is desirable to study Asia as a continent, dividing it into regions (called chunking) allows for a closer look at the many cultural and physical differences this massive land area includes.

"Chunking" the geographic regions of Asia is often a beneficial strategy to use with students. Remaining objective in this analysis is crucial. Having students formulate their own compartmentalization of Asia strengthens their understanding of the diversity in this continent.

Some study of Russia and its neighbors (mainly the one formed in 1991 as the Commonwealth of Independent States) will be offered later in this book. Therefore, most geographers accept these six regions in Asia—Central, East, Northern, Southeast, Southern, and Southwest/Western.

Skills Taught in This Unit

Map reading
- Relative location
- Use of color key/legend

Vocabulary

specialist *region*

Regions Within Asia

In this unit's study of Asia, the six regions include:

Central Asia: Kazakhstan, Kyrgyzstan, Tajikistan, Turkmenistan, and Uzbekistan

East Asia: China, Japan, Mongolia, North Korea, South Korea, and Taiwan

Northern Asia: Russia

Southeast Asia: Brunei, Myanmar, Indonesia, Cambodia (Kampuchea), Laos, Malaysia, Philippines, Singapore, Thailand, and Vietnam

Southern Asia: Afghanistan, Bangladesh, Bhutan, India, Iran, Maldives, Nepal, Pakistan, and Sri Lanka

Western/Southwest Asia: Armenia, Azerbaijan, Bahrain, Cyprus, Georgia, Iraq, Israel, Jordan, Kuwait, Lebanon, Oman, Qatar, Saudi Arabia, Syria, the United Arab Emirates, and Yemen.

Materials: screen map or large wall map of Asia, washable marker or string/yarn, removable fastener (staples, straight pins, or adhesive), "Regions in Asia" activity sheets, outline political map of Asia, pencils, colored pencils (or markers or crayons), rulers, and atlas and other reference books

Directions
Display a large map of Asia while discussing the vastness of this region. Have students speculate where to divide Asia from Europe and Africa, what to do in the Pacific Ocean to separate Asia from Oceania, what to include as Russian, and why these divisions are important. Guide students' reading and mapping of the activity sheet. Discuss and display various versions of students' maps and ask students to justify their interpretations.

Name ______________________________

Regions Within Asia

Most Asian *specialists* identify 47 countries as part of the continent. Those 47 countries are divided into six *regions*—Northern, Central, Southwest/Western, Southern, East, and Southeast. And there are some controversial areas that no one seems to know where to place.

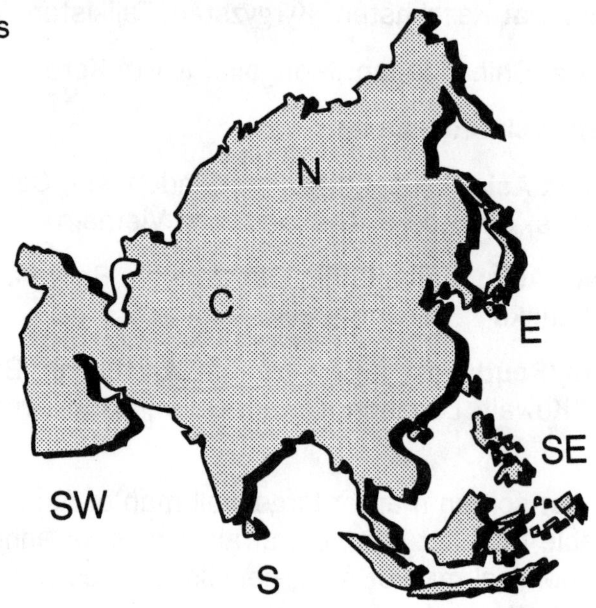

Northern Asia is Russia.

Central Asia is made up of Kazakhstan, Kyrgyzstan, Tajikistan, Turkmenistan, and Uzbekistan.

Southwest/Western Asia contains more nations than the other regions: Armenia, Azerbaijan, Bahrain, Cyprus, Georgia, Iran, Israel, Jordan, Kuwait, Lebanon, Oman, Qatar, Saudi Arabia, Syria, the United Arab Emirates, Yemen, the Sinai Peninsula portion of Egypt, and the Anatolia Peninsula of Turkey.

Southern Asia includes Afghanistan, Bangladesh, Bhutan, India, Iran, Maldives, Nepal, Pakistan, and Sri Lanka.

East Asia is comprised of China, Japan, Mongolia, North Korea, South Korea, and Taiwan.

Southeast Asia includes Brunei, Myanmar, Indonesia, Cambodia (Kampuchea), Laos, Malaysia, Philippines, Singapore, Thailand, and Vietnam.

On an Asian map, outline each of the six Asian regions using this color key:

Northern: purple	Southwest/Western: green	Southern: blue
Central: orange	East: yellow	Southeast: red

Regions of Asia

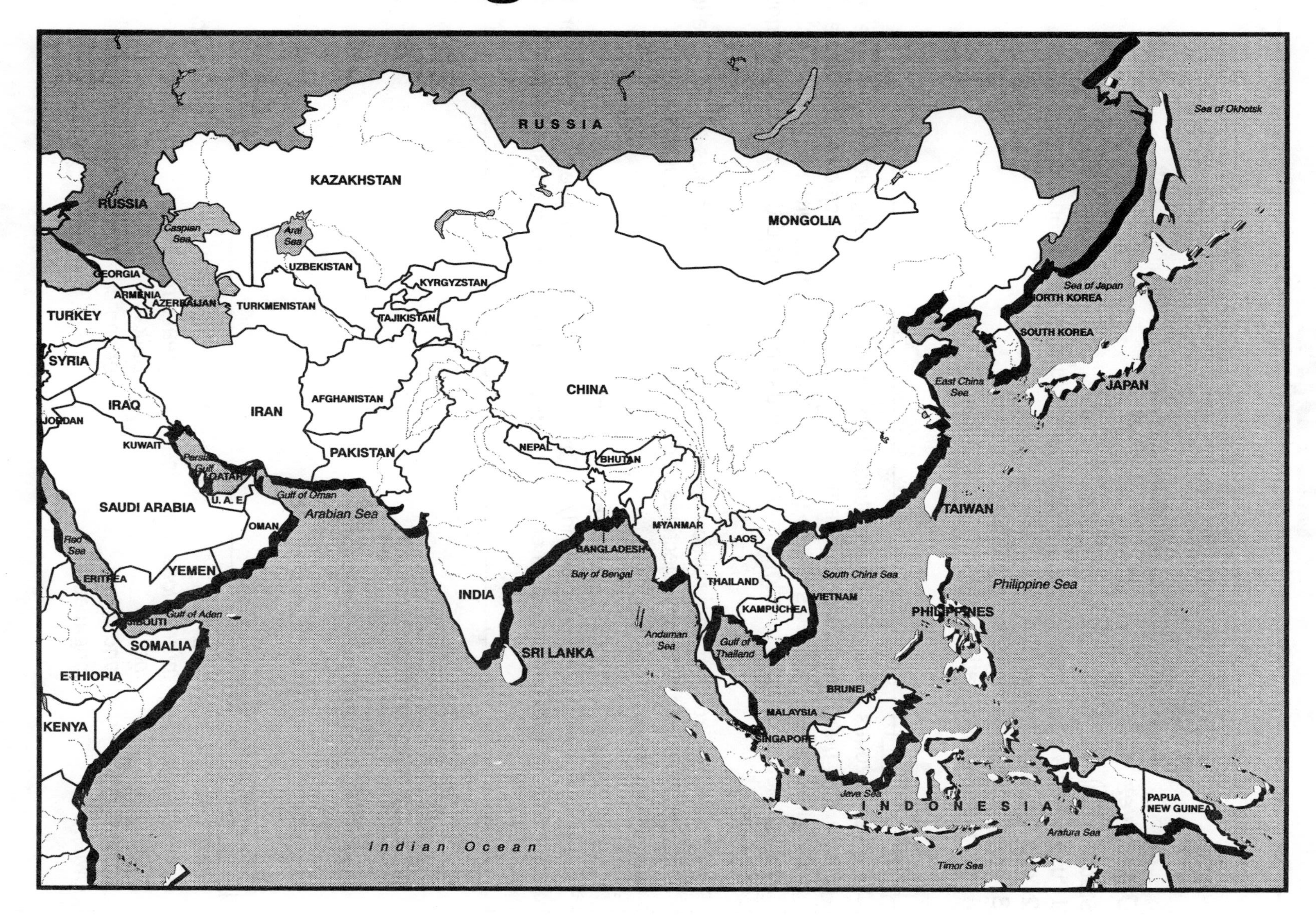

Europe

Where Is Europe?

Themes of Geography: *Location, Place, Region*

Objectives

Students will

1. use atlases and maps to identify absolute location of European cities
2. examine time zones
3. investigate great-circle route theory
4. tell the relative location characteristics of Europe

Rationale

World time zones are based on longitude lines. Every 15° of longitude equals one hour of time. The prime meridian and International Date Line are specific longitude lines used to calculate times and dates. When traveling east, add hours; when traveling west, subtract hours. Several locations in the world use nonstandard time zones for various reasons.

The great-circle route theory reinforces knowledge of the hemispheres and calculation of distance. Plane/Polar map projections and scale are sometimes taught using the great-circle route theory

Relative location for Europe is determined by physical features that are used as reference points, specifically, island/peninsula features and the proximity to water. Thousands of miles of coastline enable this region to be a world crossroads.

Skills Taught in This Unit

Map reading
- Absolute location
- Relative location

Analysis

Vocabulary

rotate	*axis*	*time zone*	*Greenwich*
prime meridian	*international date line*	*great-circle route*	*Scandinavian*
peninsula	*Iberian*	*Balkan*	*Alpine*
Jutland	*landlocked*	*ocean currents*	*uplands*
lowland	*longitude*		

Absolute Location in Europe

Many individuals have difficulty telling time and knowing that noon is 12 P.M. and that midnight is 12 A.M. Since the prime meridian is in Greenwich, England, it is sensible to conduct a study of time when studying Europe. It is also difficult for many individuals to understand the abstract beginning and ending of a 24-hour day using a progression of the world's time zones and the international date line.

Great–circle routes are the shortest distance between two points on earth. This is easily understood by using a sphere (representing earth) and a straight line (string to measure from an origin point to a destination point).

Materials: "Absolute Location in Europe" activity sheets, pencil, atlas (or other reference materials), globe, string

Directions

Discuss television scheduling of programs relating Eastern, Central, and Pacific times to the daily life of students. Review what happens with clocks and watches for noon and midnight to be identified as A.M. and P.M. Demonstrate time-telling with a globe, using 15° longitude intervals on the globe. Demonstrate how calendar dates change crossing east and west over the international date line. Guide students' reading and completion of the activity sheet. Demonstrate the great-circle route theory with several examples.

Relative Location in Europe

Europe is composed of peninsulas, a few landlocked nations, diverse landforms, and a small portion of Eurasia. Political changes continue to occur in this region, causing identification of places to be in a constant state of change. This makes studying this area both interesting and relevant to current events.

Materials: "Relative Location in Europe" activity sheets, pencil, atlas (or other reference materials), cards with the names of European nations (one nation per card)

Directions

Guide students' reading of the activity sheet. Using nation-cards sorted into groups of four or five, play a game of "landlocked or not." Have a student hold a nation-card while standing before the class. The class, playing as two teams, decides by consensus whether the student (nation) who steps forward when called upon by the teacher is "landlocked or not." Keep score of teams' accuracies and offer "homework pass," "computer pass," "media/reading pass," or "extra free-time pass" as a reward to the team with the most correct identifications.

Absolute Location in Europe

The time at various places around the world is different because the earth *rotates* on its *axis* every 24 hours. The earth rotates 360° in a day, or 15° every hour. Each of the world's *time zones* is approximately 15 longitudinal degrees wide. There are 24 standard time zones in the world.

All time zones are based on the *prime meridian*, which is located in *Greenwich*, England (a suburb of London). Because the earth rotates from west to east, the time in zones east of your location is always later than it is where you are. Traveling east, add one hour for each time zone crossed; traveling west, subtract one hour for each time zone crossed.

The *international date line* is located at 180° *longitude*, halfway around the world from the prime meridian. This imaginary line marks the difference between one day and the next. Traveling west across the date line adds a day, so going east across the date line subtracts a day.

Some locations on earth do not follow the usual lines of longitude to create time zones or dates. Countries who want all of their land area in one time zone or on one calendar date have made exceptions to the standard lines of longitude that divide time zones. Cities usually are not divided into two different zones or dates, and some nations do not follow standard time zones at all (China, India, Iran, Iraq, Myanmar, Sri Lanka, and parts of Australia and Canada).

All of Europe follows standard time zones. It is located in five different zones east of the prime meridian on the same side of the date line. If it is noon in London (near Greenwich), it is 1:00 P.M. in Rome, Italy; 2:00 P.M. in Helsinki, Finland; 3:00 P.M. in Moscow, Russia; and 4:00 P.M. in Oral (Ural'sk), Kazakhstan. If it is Saturday in London, it is Saturday in Rome, Helsinki, Moscow, and Oral (Ural'sk).

Circles divide the earth into various identifiable segments. The shortest and most direct route between two places on the earth lies along what is called a great circle. This route is called a *great-circle route*. Great-circle routes are used to navigate planes and ships around the earth. Times and dates are of no concern except at departure and arrival. Often when traveling in a short, direct great-circle route, numerous time zones are crossed. Even the date line may be crossed. Travelers usually reset their watches and calendars upon arrival at their destination.

Name ______________________

Using an atlas, give the absolute location of:

1. London, England ______________
2. Rome, Italy ______________
3. Helsinki, Finland ______________
4. Moscow, Russia ______________
5. Oral, Kazakhstan ______________
6. your town ______________

If it is 10:00 P.M. in Greenwich, England, what time is it in

7. Helsinki, Finland? ______________
8. Oral, Kazakhstan? ______________

Using an atlas, give the absolute location of:

9. Reykjavik, Iceland ______________
10. Dublin, Ireland ______________
11. Lisbon, Portugal ______________
12. Madrid, Spain ______________

If it is 5:00 A.M. in Greenwich, England, what time is it in

13. Reykjavik, Iceland? ______________
14. Madrid, Spain? ______________

15. Looking at a globe, if it is Wednesday in Europe and you are traveling from Athens, Greece, what day of the week is it in Washington, D.C., when you fly across the Atlantic Ocean? ______________
16. Still using the globe, your flight leaves Washington, D.C., and you have a layover in San Francisco, California. What happens to the day of the week? ______________
17. After getting on your San Francisco flight, you travel across the Pacific Ocean, landing in Tokyo, Japan. What day of the week is it? ______________
18. You leave Athens, Greece at 2:00 P.M. on Wednesday and land in Washington, D.C., seven time zones earlier. How is this possible? ______________
19. You leave San Francisco at 4:00 A.M. on Thursday and land in Japan on Wednesday. How is this possible? ______________
20. By measuring with a globe and a piece of string, answer the following question: Is it shorter to travel from Athens, Greece, to Tokyo, Japan, flying across the Atlantic Ocean, the United States, and the Pacific Ocean or from Athens, Greece, to Tokyo, Japan, flying in a great-circle route? ______________
21. Why is it important to know how to use a time zone map? ______________
22. Why is it important for airplanes to fly using great-circle routes? ______________

Name ______________________________

Relative Location in Europe

Europe's relative location in the heart of the Northern Hemisphere, its comprehensive coastline and its proximity to all other regions on earth are distinct advantages. Europe is often described as a *peninsula* made of peninsulas. When Europe and Asia (Eurasia) are studied as a single landmass, Europe forms its western peninsula. The south and west coasts of Europe consist of many peninsulas. Spain and Portugal form the *Iberian* Peninsula; Italy is the Italian Peninsula; and Greece is the southernmost country in the *Balkan* Peninsula. Norway and Sweden combine to form the *Scandinavian* Peninsula, and Denmark is the *Jutland* Peninsula.

Much of Europe is close to water. The region is nearly surrounded by the Atlantic Ocean and the Mediterranean, Black, North, Baltic, Norwegian, Barents, and Kara Seas. Of Europe's 40 nations, only 13 are *landlocked.* The Atlantic Ocean has a great influence on Europe's weather. Westerly winds and warm *ocean currents* cause the weather to be similar to weather in the United States. Europe's thousands of miles of coastline and navigable waterways make interaction with the rest of the world both convenient and difficult to avoid.

For ease of studying, Europe's landforms are classified into four groups—*Alpine* Mountains in the south, Central *Uplands*, North European *Lowland*, and Western Uplands. Europe's eastern boundary is formed by the Ural Mountains. Although this boundary is sometimes debated, culture, history, and geography support the Ural Mountains as the dividing line between Europe and Asia. The Ural Mountains also divide Russia into two distinctive parts, western Russia (European) and eastern Russia (Asian).

Name ______________________________

Using an atlas, give the relative location of each of these places in Europe:

1. Oslo, Norway, is located on the ______________ Peninsula. It is on the Skagerrak side of the ______________ Sea.
2. Copenhagen, Denmark, is on the ______________ Peninsula on the ______________ Sea side of Scandinavia.
3. Barcelona, Spain, was the site of the 1992 Summer Olympic Games. Barcelona is also a major industrial port on the______________Sea near the ______________ Mountains on the ______________ Peninsula.
4. Sicily is the southern island off the tip of the ______________ Peninsula in the ______________ Sea. Sardinia is the western Italian island separated from Italy by the ______________ Sea.
5. San Marino is an independent republic surrounded by the country of ______________. This nation also surrounds the State of the Vatican City which is located in the capital, ______________.
6. The Peloponnesius is a southern peninsula on the ______________ Peninsula as part of Greece. The ______________ Sea is on Greece's western side and the ______________ Sea is on its eastern side.
7. Crete is an island off the ______________ coast of Greece. It is separated from Greece by the Sea of ______________.
8. Circle the European nations from each group that are landlocked:

Poland	Switzerland	Russia	Croatia
Hungary	France	Ukraine	Bosnia
Romania	Belgium	Latvia	Macedonia
Bulgaria	Netherlands	Moldova	Albania

9. The Sierra Nevada mountain range is located on the southern Iberian Peninsula in ______________ on the ______________ Sea.
10. The Scottish Highlands are on the ______________ Isles in the political unit of ______________.
11. Ireland and ______________ are separated from the other parts of the United Kingdom (British Isles) by the ______________ Sea.
12. The ______________ Mountains divide Russia into a European and an Asian section. Kazakhstan, Georgia, Azerbaijan, and Turkey are also divided between ______________ and Asia. The ______________ Sea borders Kazakhstan, Russia, and Azerbaijan. The ______________ Sea borders Turkey, Russia, Ukraine, Romania, and Bulgaria.

How Is Europe Unique?

Themes of Geography: *Location, Place, Region*

Objectives

Students will
1. differentiate causes and effects of European climate
2. evaluate ethnic migrations in European history

Rationale

A place's climate is affected by latitude, winds and mountains, proximity to water, and ocean currents. Climate affects the inhabitants—plants, animals, and humans in significant ways. Europe's climate is often misunderstood because of its latitudinal location. England generally has a temperate climate, offering its inhabitants a variety of both opportunities and challenges.

Ethnicity creates pride and heritage. Often, political boundaries are drawn indiscriminately with no regard for the culture and history of the groups involved. Throughout European history, many different ethnic groups have migrated into this region, some peacefully, others forcefully. The diversity this has created in European history and heritage makes for an interesting European mosaic.

Skills Taught in This Unit

Map reading
- Relative location

Analysis

Vocabulary

ocean currents	*global winds*	*climate*	*westerlies*
climate factor	*flora*	*fauna*	*deciduous*
coniferous	*acid rain*	*airborne pollution*	*cause*
radioactive fallout	*effect*	*migration*	*conquest*
retreat	*Greeks*	*Romans*	*Celts*
Goths	*Visigoths*	*Vandals*	*Normans*
Anglo-Saxons	*Gaul*	*Frisians*	*Franks*
Vikings	*Huns*	*ethnicity*	*Russians*
Ukrainians	*Uzbeks*	*Kazakhs*	*Tajiks*
Georgians	*Armenians*	*Slavs*	*Byelorussians*

Physical Place Characteristics in Europe

Ocean currents and winds impacting mountains are two of five major climate factors. Climate, in turn, affects the animals and plants found on earth. These effects become both positive and negative.

Latitude, altitude, and proximity to large bodies of water cause some climatic effects on Europe. Many of Europe's physical characteristics are influenced by climate.

Materials: "Physical Place Characteristics in Europe" activity sheet, pencils

Directions
Guide students' reading of the activity sheet. A graphic organizer can be used as a prewriting activity for clarification writing that explains weather and climate or various climate factors.

Human Place Characteristics in Europe

Ethnicity is a vital component in understanding human characteristics in Europe. Many of the conflicts in this region are based on ethnic differences. Other than possibly the United States, no region in the world has the variety of ethnic groups found in Europe.

Materials: "Human Place Characteristics in Europe" activity sheets, pencils, 32 statement cards, areas of room designated: 1) British Isles, 2) Central, 3) Eastern, 4) France and Low Countries, 5) Scandinavia, 6) Southern region

Directions
Discuss the six European regions briefly (identify the countries within each region). Label areas of the room that will represent each region. Carefully guide students' reading of the activity sheet. After students have made their decisions about each statement, have various students orally read their statement cards and stand in the regional areas that are described by the statements. Discuss the influence one ethnic group had on various regions:

a. How influential were the Celts?
b. Why were the Vikings influential?
c. How could Europe be easily invaded?

Physical Place Characteristics in Europe

Europe's weather is greatly affected by *ocean currents.* There are cold deep-sea currents and warm surface currents. Surface currents are wide bands of water that are moved by *global winds* which gradually drag the water along with them. As the earth rotates on its axis, force from the spin makes currents swing to the side. The warm currents that affect Europe are the Gulf Stream, North Atlantic Drift, Norwegian Current, and North Cape Current. The cold Greenland Current affects the northern European countries of Iceland, Northern Scandinavia, and northern European Russia.

Cold and warm ocean currents affect *climate* in most parts of the world. The winds that blow over the ocean are affected by the different currents' temperatures. The Gulf Stream begins in the warm waters of the Gulf of Mexico. It flows northward along the eastern U.S. coast. At Newfoundland the Gulf Stream turns eastward and crosses the Atlantic Ocean to the British Isles. The warm winds, called *westerlies,* that accompany the Gulf Stream blow across the British Isles and Western Europe. Westerlies bring rain to many areas of Europe.

Wind and mountains become other *climate factors.* In the southern part of Western Europe, the Alps and Pyrenees mountain ranges block Atlantic winds from reaching inland Portugal, Spain, Italy, and Greece. As a result, those countries have mild, wet winters and sunny, dry summers.

Climate also affects plants *(flora)* and animals *(fauna).* Europe has always been famous for its historic forests. Today, Europe has *deciduous* (leaf) and *coniferous* (needle) forests, but they are not as widespread as they were in the past. The well-known Black Forest of southwestern Germany has been damaged in many places and destroyed in others by *acid rain.* Acid rain has killed crops and fish in Europe. *Airborne pollution* is responsible for the virtual elimination of southwestern Norway's fish population. The 1986 Chernobyl nuclear disaster in the northern Ukraine poisoned soils, plants, and animals in the Ukraine, Belarus, and Poland. Scandinavian reindeer were also affected as winds blew the *radioactive fallout* into their grazing areas.

Use the information above to complete this graphic organizer with two *causes* of climate in Europe, and two *effects* of climate in Europe.

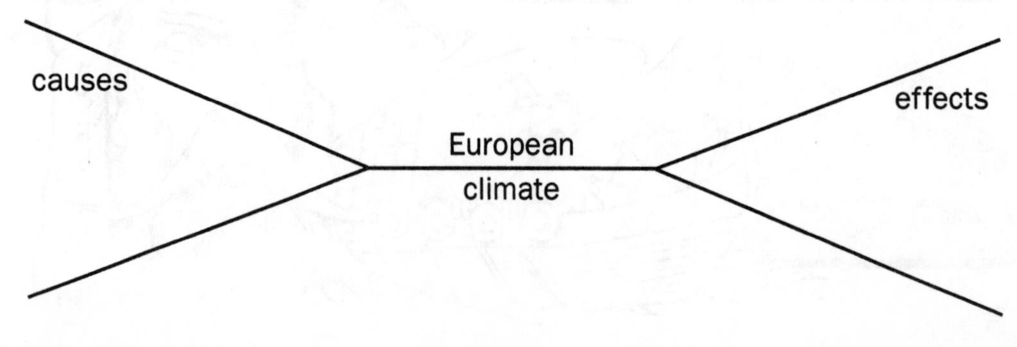

Name ______________________________

Human Place Characteristics in Europe

Europe is more of an image of human culture than of the earth's geography. Its history is the story of large- and small-scale *migrations,* triumphant *conquests,* and devastating *retreats.* Cultures and empires rose to power and fell, the process continually repeated itself throughout the course of recorded history.

Dating as far back as 2200 B.C., *Greek* civilizations flourished in Mediterranean Europe north of the Black Sea to West Asia, from North Africa into France, and across the Balkan Peninsula.

Romans, the next powerful civilization, ruled from 509 B.C., when they conquered the Greeks. *Celts* invaded the Greeks 230 years later in Delphi, Greece, in 279 B.C. The Roman civilization built an empire on the lands once held by the Greeks, from North Africa to England and from Spain to Syria. But many tribes invaded and gradually fragmented the mighty empire. Celts invaded in 390 B.C.; *Goths* invaded in the third century; *Visigoths* invaded in the fourth century; and *Vandals* invaded from North Africa in A.D. 500.

The British Isles were also in a state of change. In 800 B.C., Celts invaded from central and western Europe; in the first century, Roman armies invaded; in the fourth century, from the north, *Anglo-Saxons* invaded; and in A.D. 1066, *Normans* invaded the land. This blending of the Anglo-Saxon and Norman civilizations resulted in today's English people.

Other parts of Europe were also in turmoil. France, called *Gaul* by Celts, was invaded by both Celts and Romans; *Frisians* invaded the Netherlands and *Franks* invaded Belgium. Later, in A.D. 800, *Vikings* conquered France, Belgium, the Netherlands, and Luxembourg.

Germany, Switzerland, and Austria were invaded by Celts in 500 B.C., by Roman conquerors, and by *Huns* (Asian Mongol nomads) sweeping across Central Europe.

Southern Europe (Spain, Portugal, Italy, and Greece) was a part of both the Greek and Roman empires. Portugal and Spain became great exploring nations. They explored and settled portions of the Americas, as did the Vikings.

A major influence on the cultures of France and the Americas were the Vikings from Scandinavia (Norway, Sweden, Denmark, and Finland). They raided along the Baltic, North, and Irish Seas, and rivers of eastern and western Europe. Vikings also ventured across the Atlantic Ocean.

Eastern Europe's current *ethnicity* is a result of the nomadic history of Russian, *Ukrainian, Byelorussian, Uzbek, Kazakh, Tajik, Georgian,* and *Armenian* peoples. Eastern Europeans are predominately (75%) ancestors of *Slavs.* Their ethnic group ranking by greatest size is Russian, Ukrainian, and Uzbek.

Despite frequent attempts to unify Europe, its tumultuous and ethnically diverse past has been, and continues to be, an obstacle difficult to overcome.

Name ______________________

Decide which region of Europe is described by each historical statement.

1. The Vikings were from this region. ______________________
2. The Vandals invaded this region in 500 B.C. ______________________
3. The Celts invaded Delphi about 279 B.C. in this region. ______________________
4. The Celts invaded this region about 800 B.C. ______________________
5. The Celts invaded this region about 500 B.C. ______________________
6. The Celts called this place Gaul. ______________________
7. The Celts invaded this region in 390 B.C. ______________________
8. Russians are the largest ethnic group in this region. ______________________
9. Ancient Greeks existed from 2200 B.C. in this region. ______________________
10. The Goths invaded this region in the third century. ______________________
11. Slavs are an ethnic group in this region. ______________________
12. Frisians invaded the Netherlands in this region. ______________________
13. Invaders from this region raided along seas and rivers in Europe. ______________________
14. Explorers from this region settled in the Americas. ______________________
15. The Visigoths invaded this region in the fourth century. ______________________
16. The Anglo-Saxons invaded this region after the Celts and Romans. ______________________
17. The Huns from central Asia invaded this region after the Romans. ______________________
18. Ukrainians are the second largest ethnic group in this region. ______________________
19. France and the Americas were influenced by this region. ______________________
20. The Romans conquered the Greeks in this region. ______________________
21. The Normans invaded this region, blending with the Anglo-Saxons. ______________________
22. The Franks invaded this region. ______________________
23. The Romans invaded this region after the Celts and before the Huns. ______________________
24. The Vikings invaded this region in A.D. 800. ______________________
25. Portugal and Spain were great exploring nations from this region. ______________________
26. Uzbeks are the third largest ethnic group in this region. ______________________
27. This region had been part of the Greek and Roman empires. ______________________
28. Armenians are an ethnic group in this region. ______________________
29. The ancient Romans existed in this region from 509 B.C. ______________________
30. Georgians are an ethnic group in this region. ______________________
31. Byelorussians are an ethnic group in this region. ______________________
32. Kazakhs are an ethnic group in this region. ______________________

How Does Interaction Affect Europe?

Themes of Geography: *Location, Place, Interaction, Movement, Region*

Objectives

Students will

1. analyze trading in the European Union
2. make inferences using a database
3. create a proposal to conduct a debate and mock voting
4. assess impact of environmental pollution

Rationale

Various international trade organizations have existed in Europe. The Common Market has evolved into the European Union. The EU is a collective name for three organizations—the European Community (Common Market), the European Coal and Steel Community, and the European Atomic Energy Community. These organizations, along with the European Free Trade Association, Organization for Economic Cooperation and Development, and the Organization for Security and Cooperation in Europe, try to steer European economies toward beneficial paths. By using a simple database of trade information, students can begin to search, sort, and even query necessary information offered in a technological society.

Humans have often behaved as though many natural resources are free because there is no immediate price to pay for their use. The twentieth century alone has taught us that payment has come due for many, and permanent payment has been made for some. Europe's environments and resources present many opportunities for the study of human contact and interaction.

Skills Taught in This Unit

Map reading	Analysis	Database	Composition
Relative location		Search	
Use of color key/legend		Sort	

Vocabulary

charter	*Lomé Convention*	*currency*	*pollution*
toxic	*carbon monoxide*	*sulfur dioxide*	*smog*
acid rain	*nitrogen*	*windbreak*	

Movement of Trade in Europe

Economic trade unions have existed throughout European history. As the goals of the European Union become firmly established, Europe may be more unified with fewer restrictions than ever before.

Databases are a technological necessity. Whether using computerized or paper-and-pencil versions, students must master searching and sorting skills.

Materials: "Movement of Trade in Europe" activity sheets, pencils, yellow colored pencils (or markers or crayons), Optional: computer with database software, graph paper, rulers, colored pencils

Directions
Guide students' reading of the activity sheet, discussing the initial question. Additional possibilities include having students place export percentages into ascending or descending order and creating bar graphs from the information provided.

Air Pollution in Europe

Pollution is probably humans' greatest negative impact on the environment. Pollution in Europe is considered to be among the worst on earth. Corrective and preventative measures are coming too late for some of the world's most treasured areas.

Materials: "Air Pollution in Europe" activity sheets, pencils

Directions
Discuss with students how humans create environmental pollution. Divide the class into small groups. Each group reads the activity sheet together and decides by consensus which scenario statements are strengths, weaknesses, opportunities, or threats. Compile a chart of each group's choices and review the rationale of each group. Assign students the task of developing a plan to prevent acid rain.

Name ____________________

Movement of Trade in Europe

Is the "United States of Europe" in the development stages? Many economists, politicians, and geographers say "yes." Since the European Community (Common Market), the European Coal and Steel Community, and the European Atomic Energy Community joined together in 1994 to emerge as the European Union (EU), many feel a dramatic change in Europe is taking place.

Twelve *charter* member nations, including Germany, France, United Kingdom, Spain, Portugal, Italy, Greece, Ireland, Denmark, Belgium, the Netherlands, and Luxembourg, have been joined by Austria, Finland, and Sweden as members of the EU. Norway considered joining, but voted against it in 1994. The *Lomé Convention* also joins approximately 70 African, Caribbean, and Pacific countries into special trade agreements with the European Union.

There are no restrictions on the movement of goods, services, money, workers, and tourists among the EU nations. They share common agricultural, fishery, and nuclear research policies. They are trying to develop a common *currency* by the twenty-first century. The three main goals of the EU are: 1) to blend their economies, 2) to coordinate social developments, and 3) to bring political unity to the democratic European countries.

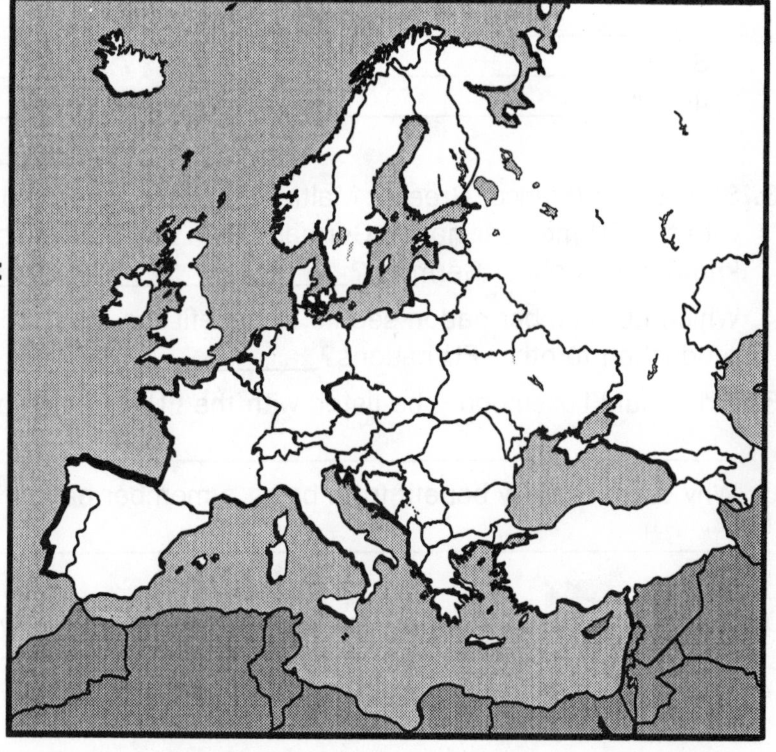

On the European map, color the 15 European Union member nations yellow.

Name ______________________________

This database chart below shows several European nations' economic relationship with their primary trading partner—the European Union. The chart shows the percent of each country's total exports that are traded with the EU.

Country	Percent	Country	Percent	Country	Percent
Austria	64	Hungary	39	Portugal	76
Belgium*	76	Iceland	68	Romania	36
Denmark	54	Ireland	75	Slovenia	54
Finland	53	Italy	53	Spain	71
France	66	Malta	56	Sweden	56
Germany	48	Netherlands	77	Switzerland	56
Greece	51	Norway	49	United Kingdom	57
		Poland	43		

* Trading partner with Luxembourg

Use the chart and map to answer these questions.

1. How many of the European Union member nations trade with other countries in the EU?

   ____

2. Name the nine non-EU nations that have a European Union member nation as their main trading partner:

   1. ____________________ 5. ____________________
   2. ____________________ 6. ____________________
   3. ____________________ 7. ____________________
   4. ____________________ 8. ____________________
   9. ____________________

3. Six nations (France, Greece, Malta, the Netherlands, Poland, and Slovenia) trade more with the EU member nation Germany than any other. What would you speculate from knowing this about Germany? ______________________________

4. Which EU member nation seems to benefit the most from exporting 76 percent of its production to other EU nations? ______________________________

5. Why would Luxembourg be listed with the EU's trading partners for Belgium? __________

   ____

6. Why could Norway benefit from being a member nation in the European Union? _______

   ____

On a separate sheet of paper, draft a proposal to the Norwegian legislature either supporting or opposing Norway's joining the European Union.

Air Pollution in Europe

One of the negative interactions between humans and the environment is air *pollution.* Nowhere in the world is this more evident than in Europe. Air pollution exists as *smog, toxic* chemicals, *carbon monoxide, sulfur dioxide*, and *acid rain.*

Acid rain is created when *nitrogen* and sulfur dioxides combine with moisture in the atmosphere. The contamination of this pollution is spread not only by the rain, snow, or hail that falls to the earth's surface but also in a dry state or as fog suspended over the landscape. Acid rain destroys animals, injures animal and plant life in lakes, damages crops and forests, endangers marine life in coastal water, pollutes rivers, erodes architecture and structures, contaminates drinking water, and causes respiratory problems for humans.

Great Britain's power plants are responsible for 9-12 percent of the air pollution in Scandinavia, particularly in Norway. The use of geothermal energy (the heat inside the earth) could cut down on the pollution and still produce needed energy. Only about 12 percent of Sweden's air pollution comes from Swedish sources. The rest comes from neighboring nations such as Germany and Poland. Austria, Bulgaria, and Slovenia estimate that about 25 percent of their forests have suffered some damage. In Germany, particularly in the Black Forest mountain region and in the Bohemian Forest, the forest damage estimates reach approximately 50 percent. Poland's forest damage is considered to be some of the worst in Europe, with about 75 percent showing some damage. Art works in Italy and Greece, even those located indoors, show signs of air pollution damage. Lakes and forests that cover almost 7,000 square miles in southern Norway are so acid polluted that the lakes no longer support fish and the forests show increasing damage.

Three solutions to air pollution, especially acid rain, offer plausible solutions to the problem. One is to control the source of the pollution, which is the use of certain fossil fuels and emissions from industries. Burning only coal or oil that has a lower level of sulfur or removing sulfur from the coal that has high levels of sulfur can help accomplish this. Some European nations are trying to implement ways of preventing air pollution. The United Kingdom has lowered its air pollution levels in the past few years. Chemical industries in Germany have been placed under stricter guidelines. Denmark has planted coastal forests to serve as *windbreaks*. Poland and the Baltic States are receiving financial help from Scandinavian countries for environmental improvements, especially in air and water quality. Iceland remains one of the world's most pollution-free environments.

Name ______________________________

We're forming a S.W.O.T. team to assess strengths (S), weaknesses (W), opportunities (O), and threats (T) in Europe's environment. Use the following to assess each scenario and circle your choices. Be prepared to defend them.

Strength (S): a positive act being done to protect or preserve the environment
Weakness (W): a negative thing that is harmful or destructive to the environment
Opportunity (O): a hopeful chance to change or improve the environment
Threat (T): a warning that predicts the possibility of damage done to the environment

S W O T 1. Factories belch chemical-laden smoke.
S W O T 2. Geothermal energy in use.
S W O T 3. Burning lignite, or brown coal, produces sulfur dioxide emissions.
S W O T 4. Oil spill off the Shetland Islands in the North Sea.
S W O T 5. Use of unleaded gasoline in cars and trucks.
S W O T 6. Stiffening security requirements in chemical industries.
S W O T 7. Listing sites and contents at nuclear waste sites.
S W O T 8. Nine out of ten children in some cities suffer from respiratory tract problems.
S W O T 9. Ban on hunting minke whales.
S W O T 10. Establishing "quiet zones" to prevent low-flying aircraft and snow-mobiles in nature preserves
S W O T 11. Governments buying back farmlands to convert to natural habitats.
S W O T 12. Use of bottled water.
S W O T 13. Placing taxes on energy and carbon dioxide emissions.
S W O T 14. Creating a multi-national park along floodplain areas.
S W O T 15. Use of natural gas instead of coal and oil.
S W O T 16. Rise in the number of endangered species.
S W O T 17. Runoff of animal manures and fertilizers from farmlands.
S W O T 18. Pollution monitoring stations placed in some areas.
S W O T 19. Thyroid tumors in children are the first proof of cancer resulting from Chernobyl nuclear reactor explosion.

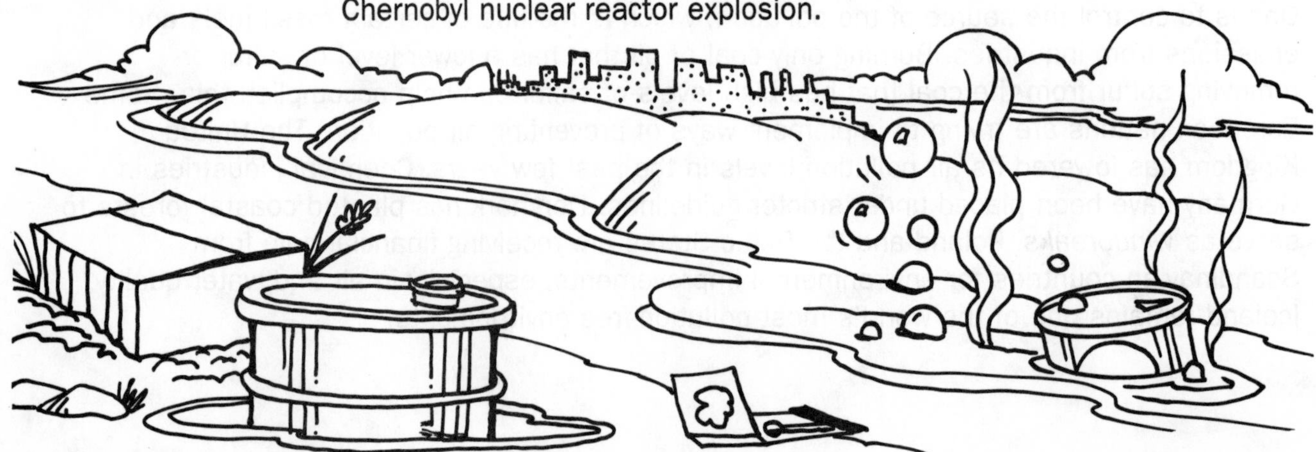

What Are the European Regions?

Themes of Geography: *Location, Place, Region*

Objectives

Students will

1. identify and locate regions within Europe
2. examine cultural versus geographical regions in Europe

Rationale

There are many cultural implications and preferences involved when dividing Europe into regions. Since World War II, the breakup of the former Soviet Union, and all the changes that have taken place in Yugoslavia, it is sometimes confusing and difficult to neatly define Europe into regions. Some Mediterranean islands are sometimes forgotten, and Greenland is often associated with North America. A geographical division of Europe is more sensible and manageable for adolescents until they have a better grasp of European history and culture.

Skills Taught in This Unit

Map reading
- Relative location
- Use of color key/legend

Vocabulary

regions
Benelux
Thrace
Tito
Nordic
Kaliningrad

Regions Within Europe

Central: Austria, Germany, and Switzerland

Eastern: Albania, Belarus, Bosnia and Herzegovina, Bulgaria, Croatia, Czech Republic, Hungary, Latvia, Lithuania, Macedonia, Moldova, Montenegro, Poland, Romania, Russia (west of the Ural Mountains), Serbia, Slovakia, Slovenia, Ukraine, and parts of Azerbaijan, Georgia, Kazakhstan, and Turkey (west=Thrace)

Northern: British Isles, Denmark, Greenland, Estonia, Finland, Iceland, Norway, and Sweden

Southern: Corsica, Greece, Italy, Malta, Portugal, Crete, Sardinia, Sicily, and Spain

Western: Belgium, France, and the Netherlands.

Russia should be studied as part European and part Asian. Update any changes occurring in Eastern Europe, since this is one of the most changing and volatile regions in the world today. Cultural geography creates much confusion in Europe. Some clarity can be gained by reinforcing European history as its geography is taught.

Materials: "Regions Within Europe" activity sheet, blank outline political map of Europe, colored pencils (or markers or crayons)

Directions
Carefully guide students' reading of the activity sheet. Note with students the overlapping of Europe with Russia and Asia.

Regions Within Europe

Europe can be divided into *regions* geographically or culturally. When the division is geographic, locations on the earth are used as a way to distinguish one area from another. Europe's geographical regions include:

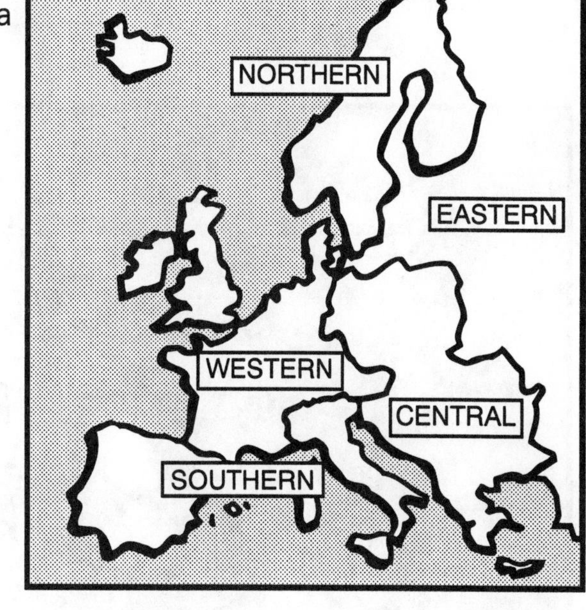

Northern: Norway, Sweden, Finland, Estonia, Denmark, British Isles, Iceland, and Greenland.

Central: Germany, Switzerland, and Austria.

Eastern: Russia, Latvia, Lithuania, Belarus, Poland, Ukraine, Slovakia, Czech Republic, Hungary, Romania, Moldova, Bulgaria, Macedonia, Albania, Montenegro, Bosnia and Herzegovinia, Croatia, Slovenia, Serbia, parts of Kazakhstan, Georgia, Azerbaijan, and Turkey.

Southern: Greece, Italy, Portugal, Malta, Sicily, Spain, and various territorial islands (Corsica, Crete, Sardinia, and Sicily).

Western: Belgium, France, and the Netherlands.

Cultural divisions are more complex than geographical divisions. Lines are drawn according to race and human social patterns—language, religion, politics, commerce. When the USSR collapsed, Chechnya began a bloody struggle for independence. *Kaliningrad* also initiated a move for independence from Russia. The former Yugoslavia, once modeled after Stalinist communism, was catapulted into civil war as a result of ethnic friction and a general lowering of economic standards in the ten years after the death of *Tito*. To date, the turmoil has resulted in the new nations of Bosnia and Herzegovinia, Croatia, Slovenia, and Macedonia. Western Turkey (*Thrace*) and the western part of Kazakhstan are European; Russia east of the Ural Mountains is European; the northeastern corners of Georgia and Azerbaijan are European.

Some of Europe's cultural regions include: **Scandinavia** (also called *Nordic*): Norway, Sweden, Denmark, Iceland, and the British Isles (U.K. and Ireland); **Mediterranean:** France, Italy, Iberian Peninsula (Spain and Portugal), Malta, Greece, and various territorial islands (Corsica, Sardinia, Sicily, and Crete); **The Low Countries and France:** Belgium, Netherlands, Luxembourg (sometimes called *Benelux*) and France; ***Baltic* States:** Latvia, Lithuania, and Estonia; ***Balkans:*** Albania, Bulgaria, Greece, Romania, Turkey, Bosnia and Herzegovinia, Croatia, Macedonia, Slovenia, Serbia, and Montenegro.

On the map of Europe, color the countries to place them in their regions.

Northern = purple   Western = red   Central = orange
Eastern = blue   Southern = yellow

Regions of Europe

North America

Where Is North America?

Themes of Geography: *Location, Place, Region*

Objectives

Students will

1. identify absolute location using various forms of identification
2. examine Florida's highest point
3. survey and name the relative location of North American places

Rationale

North America includes Canada, the United States, Mexico, and Middle America. Middle America is often called Central America or even Latin America.

Numerous methods are used to identify absolute location in addition to using latitude and longitude. Three ways are reviewed briefly in this lesson. Of the three ways, two are used worldwide—the mail and telephone systems of identification.

Many unique features are found among the locations of North America. As seen elsewhere in the world, some features are shared with other world regions. The diversity of North America's geography has influenced the diversity in the lives of its people.

Skills Taught in This Unit

Globe and map reading:
- Absolute location
- Relative location
- Use of township identifications
- Use of ZIP Codes
- Use of area codes

Analysis

Computation
- Time
- Decimals

Vocabulary

land survey system	*ZIP Code*	*area code*	*township*
Northwest Ordinance	*range*	*Calling Zone*	*prefix*
altitude	*panhandle*	*topographical map*	*isthmus*
gorge	*windward*	*coral*	*source*
relief map			

Absolute Location in North America

Many people believe that absolute location consists solely of latitude and longitude coordinates. However, there are other methods that are used worldwide to identify specific locations on the earth.

The United States is one of many nations that uses telephone and mail codes to pinpoint locations for communication services. In the past, and even today in certain locales, the township-and-range system is often considered the best logistical way to give land ownership absolute location.

Topography and relief are easily taught as absolute location. Topographic maps using contour lines are useful for many hobbies and occupations.

Materials: atlas (or other reference books), "Absolute Location in North America" activity sheets, pencil, tape or chalk, small papers numbered 1-36, postal envelopes with various ZIP Codes and some without ZIP Codes, telephone directories from various places, telephone (play or real—rotary, if possible, and touch-tone), play money ($1, $5, $10, $20 amounts) totaling about $1500, small envelopes for each student, a gavel or wooden mallet, auction tally paper, grid paper showing township's sections divided into half-section to quarter-quarter section

Directions
Using tape or chalk on the floor (or use the tiles if the floor is covered with square linoleum tiles), label 36 square township sections. Label #16 for education and #8, 11, 26, and 29 for government. Use postal envelopes with ZIP Codes and some without ZIP Codes to demonstrate the ease of sorting using ZIP Coded envelopes. Use a telephone directory (and possibly an actual telephone) to demonstrate dialing long distance numbers using prefix numbers.

Discuss the different ways to identify absolute location on the earth—grid systems using latitude/longitude; alphabet/numbers; and addresses. Ask students to describe systems they believe are not often thought of as showing absolute location. Guide students' reading and answering of the activity sheet.

Using a township grid on the floor, conduct a land auction. Values should be consistent with 1800s prices. Sell land divided into parcels of 40 to 640 acres in one section of a township. For $1.00 per acre, a student may buy a whole section at $640. Divide the section into plots of a half section (320 acres), quarter section (160 acres), half-quarter section (80 acres), and quarter-quarter section (40 acres). Give each student a presorted amount of money in a sealed envelope. Make certain no one receives less than $40. One or two students should get $640. Ask each student to point out on the grid the amount of land he or she can buy with the amount in the envelope.

Discuss after the auction:

a. How did it feel to have the original amount of money you were given?
b. How easy/difficult was it to purchase acreage, especially in the numbered section you desired or the amount of land you wanted?
c. Was the auction conducted fairly? Why or why not?
d. What might have been the circumstances in 1788 west of the Appalachians that would have made you want to participate in this auction?

Relative Location in North America

Different locations throughout North America are often distinguished by their unique features. To determine these locations, one must know exactly what is included in North America.

Generally, geographers consider North America to include Mexico and Middle America. Identify Latin America and discuss why the locations south of the Rio Grande River carry this identification.

Materials: atlases or large map of North America, "Relative Location in North America" activity sheet, pencils

Directions
Using a large-scale map of North America, discuss various interpretations of which countries are included in North America. Review the islands also included in this region (Greenland, Bermuda, Hawaii, Greater Antilles, Lesser Antilles). Guide students' reading of the activity sheet. Tell students that in the "This Is in North America" scrambled-word activity, the first letter given in each scrambled clue is actually the first letter of the answer.

Absolute Location in North America

In addition to using latitude and longitude to give absolute location, the United States has used other forms of location identification throughout its history. The *land survey system*, postal *ZIP Codes*, and telephone *area codes* are three different ways to describe a place's position.

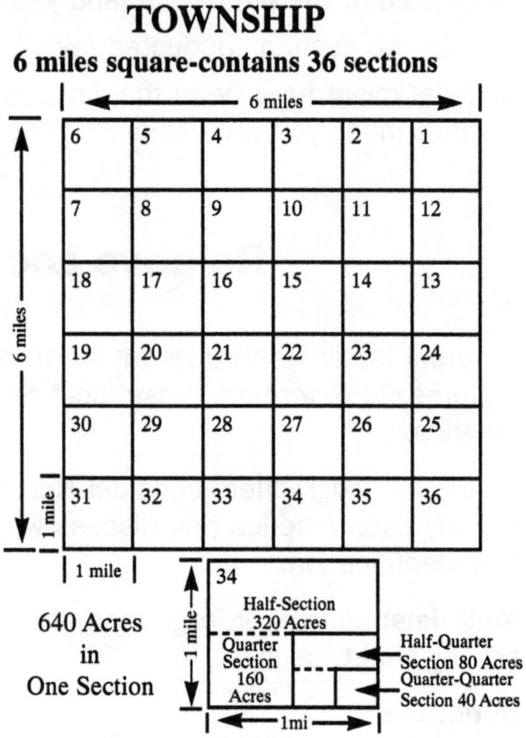

Thomas Jefferson helped design the land survey system before 1800. It is often called the *township-and-range* land-division system. By 1785, the *Northwest Ordinance* (the Ordinance of 1785) divided much of the United States west of the original 13 colonies into six-mile-square townships. Each township contained 36 sections, with 640 acres in one section. The one-square-mile sections could then be divided into 40- to 320-acre smaller sections. Education was supported by the proceeds of section 16, which was reserved for a school. Sections 8, 11, 26, and 29 were reserved for the U.S. government. As the United States was settled west of the Appalachians, a symmetrical location pattern developed across the landscape. *Topographical maps* representing surface features and *relief maps* showing differences in elevation have also been used in determining absolute location.

TOWNSHIP

6 miles square-contains 36 sections

6 miles

6	5	4	3	2	1
7	8	9	10	11	12
18	17	16	15	14	13
19	20	21	22	23	24
30	29	28	27	26	25
31	32	33	34	35	36

6 miles
1 mile
1 mile

640 Acres in One Section

34
Half-Section 320 Acres
Quarter Section 160 Acres
Half-Quarter Section 80 Acres
Quarter-Quarter Section 40 Acres
1 mile
1mi

The U.S. Postal Service introduced the ZIP Code system in 1963 to speed the sorting and delivery of mail. Five digits are used in the basic Zoning Improvement Plan (ZIP). The first digit identifies one of ten geographic areas in the United States. The second two digits identify a sectional center or large city. The last two digits identify a delivery unit or small-town delivery point. In 1983, a voluntary nine-digit ZIP Code was introduced. Any business using the extra four digits receives a discount on its mailing rate. Also, in 1963, the Postal Service introduced two-letter abbreviations for all 50 states. The change shortens the line on a mailing address where the city, state, and ZIP Code are given. These abbreviations are also used as another method for identifying location. As the United States continues to grow in population, ZIP codes increase by about 380 each year.

Telephone area codes provide a *Calling Zone* for a geographic area. These calling zones affect how a local telephone company gives local and long distance services to its customers. Access to Calling Zones all over the United States and the world requires *prefix* codes, the first three digits of a telephone number. Several states in the United States have only one area code. States with larger land areas and larger populations have numerous area codes. When dialed into a telephone system, these codes provide the specific location of the telephone that is being called. International calls often have numbers for countries and for some cities in larger countries with larger populations.

Name ____________________

Use one location in Florida to examine different absolute location types. This location is Florida's highest point, at 345 feet *altitude.* It is northeast of Paxton in Walton County in the *panhandle* of northwest Florida, less than one mile from the Florida-Alabama state line. The latitude is 30°97' N and the longitude is 86°38' W. The township identification is Sec.30, T6N, R20W. The mailing address is Paxton, FL 32538. To telephone, use area code 904. The location is in the Central Time Zone.

Using an atlas,

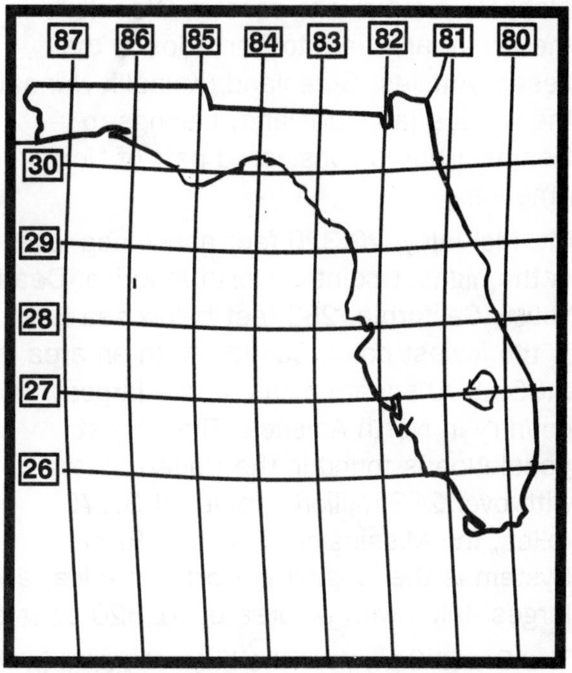

1. estimate this location on the map of Florida.

87 86 85 84 83 82 81 80
30
29
28
27
26

2. Florida's capital, Tallahassee, is located at 30°25'N. 84°17'W. Which is closer to the Atlantic Ocean—Paxton or Tallahassee?
   ____
3. How do the "N" and "W" in the latitude and longitude relate to the "N" and "W" in the township identification? __________
   ____
4. This section 30 is in which township? __________ and which range? __________
5. Alabama, Florida, Georgia, Mississippi, and Tennessee are in the ZIP Code geographic area that begins with 3. Which is the southernmost of these five states? ______
   ____
6. What is Florida's two-letter postal abbreviation? ____
7. If the following Florida cities are in these area codes, which is in the same Calling Zone as Paxton? (Circle one.)
   Miami-303 Orlando-407 Tampa-813 Pensacola-904
8. If it is 12 P.M. Eastern Time in the remainder of Florida, what time is it in Paxton?
   ____
9. Florida's topography is described as flat or rolling; its highest point is ____ feet in the NW. What is the intermediate direction abbreviated as NW? __________
10. If there are approximately 3.28 feet in one meter, what is Florida's highest point's altitude in meters? ____________________
11. Which states border Florida on the north? ____________________

Relative Location in North America

North America extends from north of the Arctic Circle at Greenland, through the 48 contiguous United States, through Mexico, and across the *isthmus* of Middle America to Panama's southern border. North America stretches west to east from Attu Island in Alaska's Aleutians to eastern Greenland in the north, and east to Barbados in the Lesser Antilles. Greenland (Kalaallit Nunaat), the world's largest island, belongs to Denmark but is considered part of North America.

Mt. McKinley, 20,320 feet above sea level, is the highest point in North America. Death Valley, California, 282 feet below sea level, is the lowest point. Canada, with an area of 3,850,000 square miles, is the largest country in North America. The largest population is found in the United States, with over 263 million people. At 3,170 miles, the Mississippi/Missouri River System is the longest in North America, and Lake Superior (shared by both countries) is the largest lake, with an area of 31,820 square miles.

The Grand Canyon is the biggest *gorge* in the world with a depth of over one mile. California's redwoods are the tallest trees; its giant sequoias are the largest trees; and its bristlecone pines are the oldest living things. Hawaii's Mount Waialeale is the world's rainiest place. It rains 350 days a year, for an annual average rainfall of 460 inches.

Canada and the United States share the longest (5,000-mile) unfortified border in the world. It consists of the Alaska/Canada (1,250-mile) border and the U.S. contiguous states/Canada (3,987-mile) border. They share other features as well, such as the Canadian Shield, the Rocky Mountains, the Great Lakes, the Columbia River, and Niagara Falls.

Latin America extends south from the Rio Grande River (between the United States and Mexico). Mexico's territories once extended farther north, which explains the U.S. border states' strong Spanish ties. Mexico has the largest Spanish-speaking population in the world.

Middle America includes the seven nations located between Mexico and South America. The Panama Canal, also in Middle America, provides a shortcut between the Atlantic and Pacific Oceans. The islands of the West Indies (Greater Antilles and Lesser Antilles) separate the Caribbean Sea and the Atlantic Ocean. The Bahamas are located in the Atlantic Ocean. Bermuda, another North American island, is located 650 miles off the North Carolina coast.

Name ______________________________

Here are some scrambled locations in North America. See if you can unscramble the letters, using the clue "This is in North America . . . ."

Scrambled	Clue
M C I X O E	1. It is not Canada or the United States
S R P O U E I R	2. It is the world's second largest as well as the highest and deepest of the five.
G A N E D R E N L	3. It is really a "bowl filled with ice" that belongs with Europe.
B O D A S R A B	4. It is the easternmost Caribbean island.
N A R A I G A	5. You do not have to tumble over it in a barrel.
M E N C L I Y K	6. It soars above like its Indian name—*Denali*, which means "high one"
W E E A A A L L I	7. It is located on the Pacific-drenched *windward* side of Kauai.
B U D E M A R	8. Its *coral* beaches belong with Europe.
B S M H A A A	9. Columbus first landed here in the Atlantic, finding no rivers and not finding "India."
P M N A A A	10. It is a link between oceans and continents.
C D N A A A	11. It is known for its size, its two official languages, its north magnetic pole, and its open border.
A L S I N E T L	12. There is a Greater and a Lesser.
D A H E T Y L E A L V	13. It is no wonder it is the lowest place in this region.
S U Q A O I E	14. It is the biggest plant California has to offer.
C U B O M A L I	15. It crosses from its *source* in Canada to join the Snake in the United States.
A A E I U L N T	16. These islands are so far west you might think they belong with Russia in Asia.
U E T N I D E T S A T S	17. It is the most populous country in this region.
R O I E R D A G N	18. It divides English- and Latin-speaking people.
R Y C K O	19. These rugged mountains span from Canada into the United States.
R O D O W E D	20. These grand and lanky California trees add color to their timber.

How Is North America Unique?

Themes of Geography: *Location, Place, Region*

Objectives

Students will

1. investigate climate
2. construct climographs
3. examine and map population distribution and density
4. infer population characteristics from a cartogram

Rationale

Climate is the weather that occurs over a long period of time in any given location. It is difficult to determine climate by region worldwide because of scarce, insufficient, and short-term records. No definitive boundary line can be drawn between one climatic region and another. Precipitation (especially rainfall) and temperature are the most reliable pieces of climatic data and can usually be obtained accurately and easily.

Climographs are graphs that show some climate information at a glance. Both a temperature line graph and a precipitation vertical bar graph are illustrated on a climograph for one location.

Skills Taught in This Unit

- Map reading
  - Relative location
  - Use of symbol and color key/legend
  - Use of cartogram
- Analysis
- Graphing
  - Climographs

Vocabulary

climate	*tropical*	*temperate*	*polar*
precipitation	*temperature*	*rain shadow*	*climograph*
line graph	*bar graph*	*Fahrenheit*	*Celsius*
population density	*megalopolis*	*metropolitan*	*proportion*
urban	*meridian*	*census*	*suburb*
cartogram			

Physical Place Characteristics in North America

An important physical place characteristic is climate. Climographs are a simple method used to illustrate temperature and precipitation at a single glance. These graphs are easily constructed using a temperature line graph in the upper portion of a climograph and a precipitation vertical bar graph in the lower portion of the same climograph.

Materials: "Physical Place Characteristics in North America" activity sheets, pencils, red and blue colored pencils (markers or crayons)

Directions
Brainstorm the definitions of and the differences between weather and climate. Lead the discussion toward weather features that determine climate. Briefly name various types of climatic regions. Guide students' reading of the activity sheet and construction of a climograph.

Human Place Characteristics in North America

North America's population characteristics include many ethnic backgrounds, a variety of living patterns, and differing population densities. A way to see those differences is with a cartogram. The cartogram is a map/graph that shows data proportionally. Some cartograms are three-dimensional.

Materials: "Human Place Characteristics in North America" activity sheets, pencils, maps of North America, colored pencils (markers or crayons), atlas (or other reference books)

Directions
Use the class as the population being studied. Discuss the class's population characteristics, ie., total number of students, gender count, ethnic makeup, density of seating arrangement. Guide students' reading of the activity sheet. Ask students to consider how to map the class's population. Then map North America's population statistics. After examining cartograms, assign students to design either a population map or a population cartogram of the class.

Physical Place Characteristics in North America

North America encompasses all types of *climate*. The *tropical* climate is found in Middle America, while a dry climate is found in Mexico and the southwestern United States. The humid *temperate* climates are found in Canada and the United States, and the *polar* climates are found in Greenland, Canada, and Alaska.

Precipitation and *temperature* are keys to understanding climate as a physical characteristic of a place. Precipitation generally declines toward the west of North America, except for the *rain shadow* effect of the Pacific Coastal strip. Temperature also tends to vary with latitude, becoming cooler the farther north one goes.

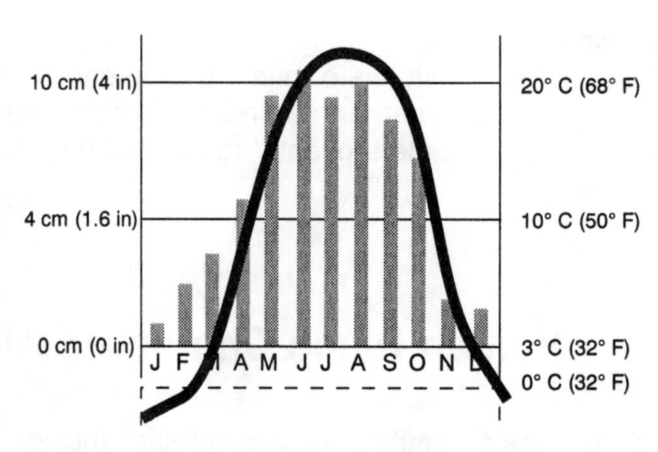

A *climograph* is used to show both temperature and precipitation. Temperature is shown on a *line graph* in the upper half of the climograph, while precipitation over the past 12 months is recorded on a vertical *bar graph* in the lower half. Many climographs use standard identification systems with names and letters recording specific climate characteristics for a given place. A range of colors is often used to illustrate the standard climate identifications.

Simple climographs are made using red to mark 12 dots which are connected to create the temperature line graph. Red is chosen because thermometers that measure temperature often show the reading in red. Blue is used to make 12 vertical bar graph columns for recording precipitation. Blue is used to symbolize water. Less complex climographs can be designed with pencil or pen on graph paper.

The 12 months of the year are printed across the bottom of the graph, from left to right, from January to December. Usually, temperature is shown on the right axis of the graph in degrees (*Fahrenheit* or *Celsius*), while precipitation is shown on the left axis in inches or centimeters.

A fill-in of coloring can be used from the temperature line graph through the precipitation vertical bar graph. Often the range of colors used to illustrate the standard climate types is used for this fill-in of coloring. It is possible that a climograph can have data that actually goes off the graph—if temperatures are so high or low or if the precipitation is beyond the numbers shown. There may also be no precipitation in some places for some climate types, in which case the graph for that month would be zero.

Name ______________________

Design a climograph, using the following temperature and precipitation data.

	Jan.	Feb.	Mar.	April	May	June	July	Aug.	Sept.	Oct.	Nov.	Dec.
Temp.	37.2	38.3	44.1	54.3	61.5	68.9	75.0	77.7	71.6	60.6	50.4	41.4
Precip.	2.0	2.6	4.3	5.3	5.9	6.3	5.6	4.6	7.5	7.2	4.3	2.3

1. Does this climate have a wet or dry winter? ______________
2. Does this climate have a wet or dry summer? ______________
3. Does this climate's warmest month average above 71.6°F? ______________
4. Does this climate's warmest month average below 71.6°F? ______________
5. Does this climate have at least one month below 32°F? ______________
6. Does this climate have all months averaging above 32°F? ______________
7. Does this place seem to be north or south of the equator? ______________
8. Does this place appear to be near the equator? ______________
9. Does this place seem to be close to an ocean? ______________

Precipitation (inches) | Temperature (°F)

Precipitation axis: 30, 28, 26, 24, 22, 20, 18, 16, 14, 12, 10, 8, 6, 4, 2, 0

Temperature axis: 100, 90, 80, 70, 60, 50, 40, 30, 20, 10, 0, -10, -20, -30, -40, -50

Months: J F M A M J J A S O N D

10. Does this place appear to be near mountains? ______________
11. This place is a humid subtropical climate type. Using an atlas, name some places in North America that have this type of climate. ______________

____

____

Write a descriptive paragraph about this place. Use the climate factors from the data and climograph. Would you want to live in this place? Why or why not?

____

____

____

____

Human Place Characteristics in North America

North America has the fourth greatest concentration of people inhabiting the earth. Eastern North America, specifically southeastern Canada and the east central United States, has the highest population density in North America.

Megalopolises, like Boston, Washington, New York, Philadelphia, and Baltimore, show major concentrations of people living in major *metropolitan* centers. Chicago, Detroit, Cleveland, San Francisco, Los Angeles, and San Diego are megalopolises found in the United States, while Montreal, Toronto, and Windsor are megalopolises found in Canada. Even St. Louis, Kansas City, Denver, Dallas, and Seattle can be included as small clusters with high population densities. *Urban* areas are where the majority of North Americans choose to live.

Over a quarter of a billion people live in Canada and the United States. North Americans from Canada, the United States, and Middle America are mostly found east of the 100th *meridian* of longitude. One of the five most populated cities in the world, Mexico City, is just east of this meridian. Add New York City, another of the world's five largest cities, to Mexico City, and North America has two of the world's greatest metropolitan areas in the world. Seven of the United States' ten largest cities (New York, Chicago, Houston, Philadelphia, Detroit, Dallas, and San Antonio) are also east of 100° West longitude. Though California is the United States' most populated state, the remaining nine of the ten most populated states (Texas, New York, Florida, Pennsylvania, Illinois, Ohio, Michigan, New Jersey, and North Carolina) are also east of the 100th meridian.

The most recent *census* in the United States showed that more than half of its citizens live in the southern and western regions. About 80 percent of U.S. citizens live in cities or *suburbs*. The United States is known as a population that includes people of different races and nationalities. Groups of Native Americans link North and Middle America to the country's population history. Hispanic, African, European, and Asian influences in the United States are melded into its greatly diverse population.

Most Canadian citizens live in the provinces of Ontario and Quebec. The British influence in Ontario and the French influence in Quebec are unmistakable. Asian and other European influences are also found in Canada.

Latin America is also an "America." However, many citizens of Latin American countries prefer to be identified with their nationalities. The influx of European settlers in the sixteenth century came from the Iberian Peninsula and France, where Latin was the official language. Mexico is the most populated of the Latin American countries in North America.

On a map of North America

1. locate the 22 cities mentioned in the reading and label each with a dot and its name.
2. Color the ten most populated states in the United States, making California a color different from the other nine.
3. Color the two Canadian provinces mentioned in the reading.

Name ______________________

A *cartogram* is a map showing information with the land areas in *proportion* to the information being given. This cartogram of North America's population gives the size of each country according to its population.

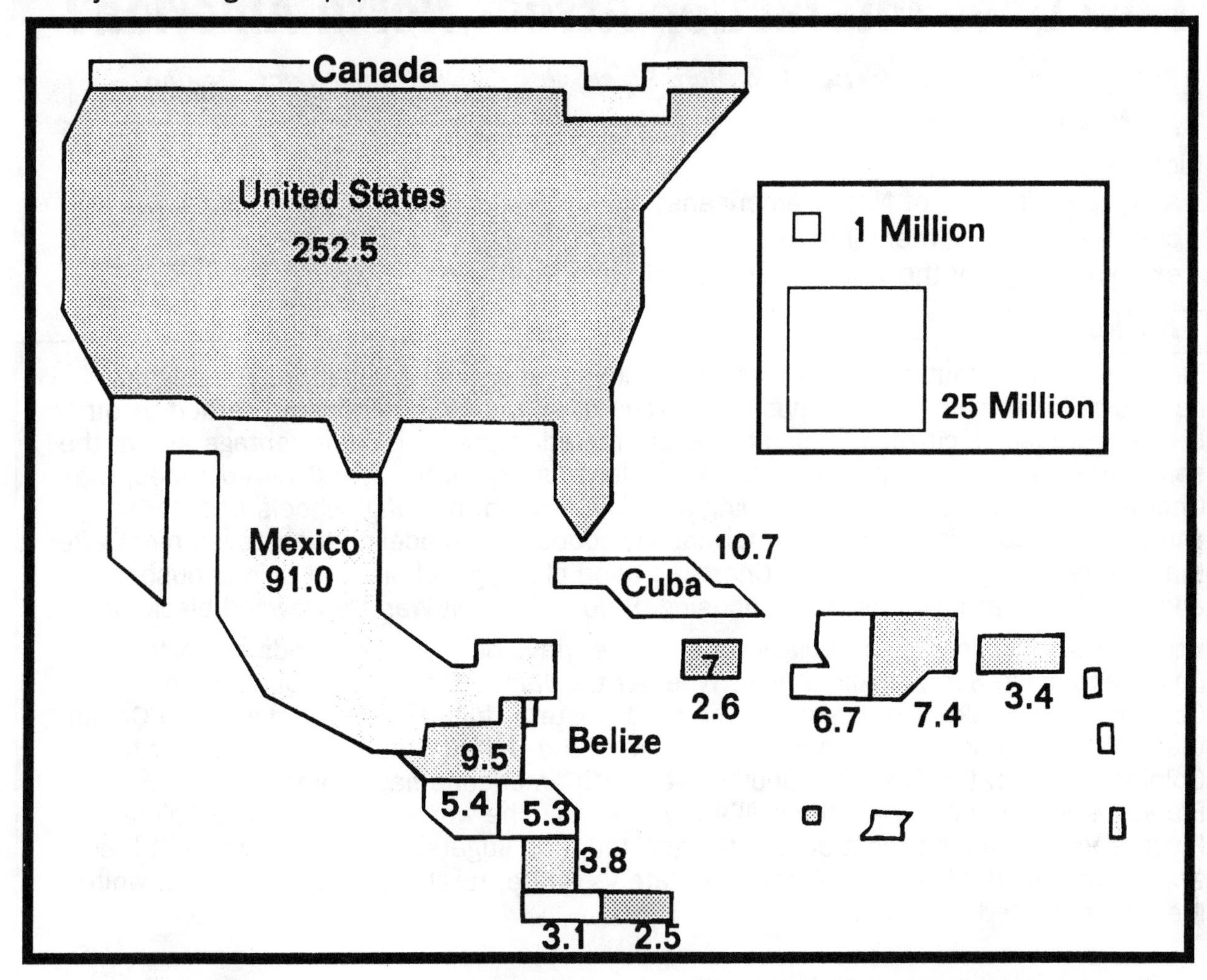

1. Guatemala
2. El Salvador
3. Honduras
4. Nicaragua
5. Costa Rica
6. Panama
7. Jamaica
8. Haiti
9. Dominican Republic
10. Puerto Rico
11. Trinidad and Tobago
12. Guadaloupe
13. Barbados
14. Netherland Antilles

Using the cartogram of North America:

4. Which nation has the largest population in the region? ______________________
5. Which is larger in population, Canada or Mexico? ______________________
6. Are any of the Caribbean Island nations as populated as Canada? ______________
7. Why would you think Greenland's population is not included on this cartogram?

____

How Does Interaction Affect North America?

Themes of Geography: *Location, Place, Interaction, Movement, Region*

Objectives

Students will
1. analyze emigration of Native Americans
2. create a historical mental map
3. examine usage of the water from the Colorado River

Rationale

Movement throughout history is divided into immigration and emigration. The original natives of North America were pushed westward, as the country became settled by other U.S. and Canadian citizens. Indian tribes attempted to preserve their heritage and at the same time become enculturated into the society. As one of the Five Civilized Tribes, the Cherokee were influential in developing a writing system, building schools and Christian churches, establishing courts with formal law codes, and modeling their government after the U.S. federal government. The Cherokee used plow agriculture and animal husbandry and had European-style dress and housing. Before the Civil War, they owned black slaves.

Environmental concerns, especially water usage, have been on the minds of North Americans since Ben Franklin's time. Whether the James Bay area of Quebec, the Columbia and Snake river system in the northwestern United States and western Canada, the Rio Grande and Rio Conchos river system of the United States and Mexico, or the Colorado River of the American Southwest, North Americans have come to believe Franklin's statement, "when the well's dry, we know the worth of water." The Colorado River is famous as the most debated, legislated, and litigated river in the world. It literally and figuratively divides North America—state vs. state, rural vs. urban, Indian vs. white, Mexico vs. United States.

Skills Taught in This Unit

Map reading
- Relative location
- Use of mental mapping

Analysis

Vocabulary

Trail of Tears	*emigration*	*Cherokee*	*Iroquois*	*Chickasaw*
Creek	*Seminole*	*John Ross*	*Chattanooga*	*Winfield Scott*
Civil War	*descendant*	*reservation*	*trust land*	*source*
Five Civilized Tribes	*salinity*	*desalination*	*vaquita*	*totaba*
American Southwest	*Grand Canyon*	*mouth*	*distinctions*	*Choctaw*
Gulf of California	*elevation*	*silt*	*semiarid*	*drainage basin*
regulation	*acre-feet*	*reservoir*	*habitat*	*Salton Sea*
Hoover Dam	*Lake Mead*	*Lake Powell*	*Imperial Valley*	*Navajo*
aqueduct	*ecosystem*	*hydroelectric*		

Emigration and the Trail of Tears

The study of the historical movement of people through emigration and immigration brings focus to ethnicity. The relocation of Native Americans created reservations and trust lands that took the place of free movement within North America.

Students retain information at more advanced levels with mental mapping than they do when preprinted maps are used. This activity will focus on mental mapping in order to reinforce the material.

Materials: "Emigration and the Trail of Tears" activity sheets, pencils, colored pencils (markers or crayons)

Directions
Discuss with students "Who are considered Americans?" Lead the discussion toward ethnic pride. Discuss with students who "Native Americans" were, making certain to include distinctions between North American, Middle American, and South American Indian groups. Distinguish *Inuit* from *Eskimo*. For example, *Inuit* means "the people." Inuits are of Asian descent. *Eskimo* is the Indian word for *Inuit*.

Water Allocation and the Colorado River

Water is one of the most precious resources on the earth. Human regulation of North America's many great river systems has created countless benefits and permanent side effects that have changed the landscape and will continue to do so.

Materials: one-gallon jug of blue-tinted water (add a drop of blue food coloring), one measuring tablespoon, "Water Allocation and the Colorado River" activity sheets, pencils

Directions
Discuss with students that water is a permanent resource. Use a gallon jug of water to illustrate all of the earth's water. Tell students that available fresh water is represented by only one tablespoon's worth from the gallon. Pour one measured tablespoon of water from the jug. Explain to students that about 97 percent of our planet's water is seawater, another 2 percent is frozen in icecaps and glaciers, and less than half of one percent of earth's total water is represented by one tablespoon of fresh water. Guide students' reading and answering on the activity sheet.

Emigration and the Trail of Tears

The *Cherokee*, North American Indians, originally lived near the Great Lakes. They were defeated by the the *Iroquois* and Delaware tribes and moved to the southeastern United States. There they lived in the mountains of the western Carolinas, northern Georgia, and eastern Tennessee. Eventually they became the largest and most powerful Native Americans in this region.

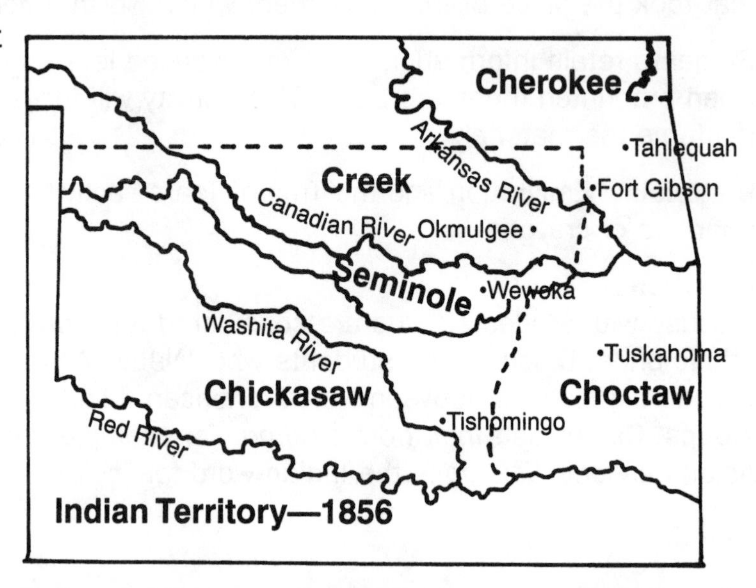

President Andrew Jackson signed the Indian Removal Act in 1830 that resulted in the Cherokee, *Chickasaw, Choctaw, Creek,* and *Seminole* (often called the *Five Civilized Tribes*) being moved to federal lands in the Western territory. People who favored this movement believed the relocation would protect the lives of Native Americans and offer tribes a chance to adjust to white culture. Little consideration was given to the fact that the five tribes were traditional enemies, although they shared many culture traits. In 1838 the Cherokee were moved north and east of the Arkansas River. The Choctaw were moved south of the Arkansas and Canadian Rivers. The Creeks were relocated north of the Canadian River and west of the Arkansas River. At first the Chickasaw were placed with the Choctaw, and the Seminoles were settled with the Creek. Later each tribe was given its own area.

A great majority of the Cherokee Nation disagreed with the treaties that were designed to send them to Arkansas and Indian Territory (now Oklahoma) in 1838-39. Led by *John Ross* (Coowescoowe), who later became chief of the United Cherokee Nation, most Cherokees made the journey called the *Trail of Tears. Chattanooga*, Tennessee, was the starting point for this sad but historic journey. More than 15,000 Cherokees were forcibly driven by General *Winfield Scott* across parts of Tennessee, Kentucky, Illinois, Georgia, Alabama, Missouri, and Mississippi into Arkansas and Oklahoma. About 4,000 Cherokees died of disease and exposure on the winding, difficult journey. Some who escaped and avoided the removal fled into the Great Smoky Mountains and eventually resettled in western North Carolina.

The land reserved for the Five Civilized Tribes did not remain theirs. After the *Civil War*, tribal lands were lost because the tribes sided with the South. By the early 1880s, tribal ownership of lands was canceled. In 1907, when Oklahoma was granted statehood, all tribal lands were opened for white settlement.

Many *descendants* of the Five Tribes live on *reservations* in Oklahoma today. Cherokees reside in California, Florida, Michigan, North Carolina, and Oklahoma. North Carolina's only Federal Indian Reservation and *Trust Land* belongs to the Cherokee. The Cherokee are the largest Native American tribe in North Carolina and Oklahoma today.

Name ______________________

A map was designed in 1836 "showing the lands assigned to EMIGRANT INDIANS west of Arkansas and Missouri." Use an atlas and the information you just read to help you design your own "mental map" of the Indian Territory in 1838-39.

1. Define *emigration.* ______________________
2. Originally, the Cherokee lived near ______________________.
3. In the southeastern United States, the Cherokee lived in the mountains of western ______________, northern ______________, and eastern ______________.
4. When resettled in the western territory, the Cherokee were to live ______________ and ______________ of the Arkansas River.
5. Today, the Cherokee live in five states: 1) ______________, 2) ______________ 3) ______________, 4) ______________, and 5) ______________.
6. The journey to relocate the Cherokees was called ______________________.
7. Coowescoowe was the Cherokee name for ______________________.
8. The Trail of Tears began in ______________________, Tennessee.

Water Allocation and the Colorado River

The Colorado River is the largest river in the *American Southwest*. People living in seven states and in Mexico use its water. The demands humans have placed on this mighty river have exceeded its capacity to support this region.

From its *source* in the Rocky Mountains, the Colorado River once flowed, unchecked, 1,450 miles through the mountain range. It carved through the *Grand Canyon* before the river's *mouth* emptied into the *Gulf of California*. Its *distinctions* made it the seventh longest river in the United States, the greatest drop in *elevation* in North America, and one of the saltiest and *siltiest* of all rivers. The *drainage basin* of the Colorado in the *semiarid* Southwest was larger than France. However, the Colorado River has been regulated to the point that now little of its water actually reaches the Gulf of California.

Regulation began in 1922 with the Colorado River Compact. The agreement divided seven western states (Wyoming, Utah, Colorado, Nevada, Arizona, New Mexico, and California) into upper and lower basins. Each state was to receive 7.5 million *acre-feet* of water a year. A 1944 treaty guaranteed Mexico 1.5 million acre-feet per year. In spite of the compact, since 1930, the Colorado has averaged only 14 million acre-feet of the 16.5 million acre-feet it was supposed to deliver, not including the 2 million acre-feet lost annually in evaporation from *reservoirs* each year.

The Colorado River provided a *habitat* for elk in Wyoming and minnows in Utah. It provided electricity for Nevada, offered recreation in Arizona, grew grapes in New Mexico, made California's *Salton Sea* basin famous, and watered cantaloupes in Mexico. It also made possible Nevada's *Hoover Dam* with *Lake Mead*, established California's *Imperial Valley* as a rich farmland, made Utah's *Lake Powell* the longest man-made lake in the United States, irrigated New Mexico's *Navajo* Indian Reservation, and provided southern California's cities with water from the Colorado River *Aqueduct*.

Negative effects of human regulation of the Colorado's flow are quite visible. While the dams provide flood control, *hydroelectric* power, recreation, and water storage, they also alter *ecosystems*—erosion in the Grand Canyon, destruction of canyons like Glen Canyon, and the threat to native species, such as the *totaba* and *vaquita*. The *salinity* level has increased to 14 times its original level. *Desalination* plants try to reclaim some of the lost drainage water. The U.S. National Park Service must limit the number of rafts in the Grand Canyon daily to prevent overcrowding.

Name ______________________________

There are hopeful signs for the Colorado River's future stabilization. New ideas and understanding provided by children, environmentalists, politicians, and ordinary citizens create an awareness of the problem. This growing awareness of water and the willingness of individuals to protect it confirms that the Colorado River may regain some of its former majesty.

1. The largest river in the American Southwest is the ______________________________.
2. The ____________ of the Colorado River is a lake in the ________________Mountains.
3. The ____________ of the Colorado River is the Gulf of ______________________________.
4. Name four distinctive traits of the Colorado River:
   a. ______________________________
   b. ______________________________
   c. ______________________________
   d. ______________________________
5. List the seven states in the United States most affected by the Colorado River:
   a. ______________________ e. ______________________
   b. ______________________ f. ______________________
   c. ______________________ g. ______________________
   d. ______________________
6. What nation shares the waters of the Colorado River with the United States?
   ____
7. The Salton Sea is located in ______________________________.
8. Lake Mead and Hoover Dam are located in ______________________________.
9. The Colorado River carved a deep, narrow valley with steep sides called the ________
   ______________________________.
10. Which Indian Reservation is located in New Mexico near the Colorado River? ________
   ____
11. Give several positive effects and negative effects the Colorado River and humans have had on the environment. ______________________________
   ____
   ____
   ____
   ____
   ____

What Are the North American Regions?

Themes of Geography: *Location, Place, Region*

Objectives

Students will
1. examine various regional identifications for North America
2. design a color-keyed map

Rationale

Due to physical geography, economics, individual perception, and contemporary changes in North America, the regions will continue to see dynamic and rapid changes.

In the lesson, Central America includes Guatemala, Belize, Honduras, El Salvador, Nicaragua, Costa Rica, and Panama. The Caribbean Islands are in two groups, Greater Antilles and Lesser Antilles. The Lesser Antilles are divided into the Leeward Islands and the Windward Islands.

Greater Antilles
Cuba
Jamaica
Hispaniola (Haiti,
Dominican Republic
Puerto Rico)
Lesser Antilles
Bahamas
Caymans

Leeward Islands
Antigua and Barbuda
Montserrat
Saba
St. Eustasius
St. Christopher (Kitt)-Nevis
Turks and Caicos
Virgin Islands
Netherlands Antilles:
Aruba
Bonaire
Curaçao

Windward Islands
Barbados
Dominica
Grenada
Guadeloupe
Martinique
St. Lucia
St. Vincent
Grenadines
Trinidad and Tobago

Skills Taught in This Unit

Map reading
- Relative location
- Use of color key/legend

Analysis

Vocabulary

Anglo-America
Islands
Interior Periphery
French Canada
territories
Dairy Belt
New England
Foundry
Latin America
Empty Quarter
West Coast
Southwest
states
Columbia Basin
Gulf
Mex-America
Middle America
Dixie
Agricultural Heartland
South
Ecotopia
Wheat Region
Pacific
New England/ Maritime Provinces
Central America
Breadbasket
Anglo-American Core
provinces
Corn Belt
North
Quebec

Regions Within North America

North America is more than Canada and the United States of America. Latin America is more than Mexico and Central America. For purposes of this study we include both in North America.

Canada
United States of America
Mexico
Central America including Belize, Costa Rica, El Salvador, Guatemala, Honduras, Nicaragua, Panama
Caribbean Islands including

Greater Antilles
Cuba
Jamaica
Hispaniola (Haiti,
Dominican Republic
Puerto Rico)
Lesser Antilles
Bahamas
Caymans

Leeward Islands
Antigua and Barbuda
Montserrat
Saba
St. Eustasius
St. Christopher (Kitt)-Nevis
Turks and Caicos
Virgin Islands
Netherlands Antilles:
Aruba
Bonaire
Curaçao

Windward Islands
Barbados
Dominica
Grenada
Guadeloupe
Martinique
St. Lucia
St. Vincent
Grenadines
Trinidad and Tobago

Materials: "Regions Within North America" activity sheet, colored pencils (markers or crayons), map of North America

Directions
Brainstorm with students why some regions have overlapping names and identifications. Guide students' reading and mapping of North America's regions.

Regions Within North America

Anglo-America and *Latin America* are the two major regional divisions used to differentiate between cultures in North America. However, Mexico, Central America, and the Caribbean Islands are more accurately combined into a region called *Middle America*.

Middle America is studied in combination with the United States and Canada, and is called the North American region.

Middle America includes Mexico, *Central America*, and the Caribbean Islands. All of these places are usually studied with the North American region.

Canada and the United States (Anglo-America) share a number of subregions. The *Interior Periphery* is the largest. Some of the *West Coast*, the *Agricultural Heartland*, the *Anglo-American Core*, and the *New England/Maritime Provinces* are in both nations. Canada also has a subregion called *French Canada*. Unique to the United States are the *Southwest* and the *South*.

There are other ways to subdivide North America. Some use political names (Canada's *provinces* and *territories*, the United States' *states*, Mexico's states). Some use agricultural names (the *Corn Belt*, the *Dairy Belt*, the *Columbia Basin*, *Wheat Region*). Some use perceptions (the *North*, *New England*, the *Gulf*, the *Pacific*). Some use the "Nine Nations" (*Quebec*, the *Foundry*, *Dixie*, the *Breadbasket*, *Mex-America*, the *Islands*, New England, the *Empty Quarter*, *Ecotopia*).

Color the regions of North America on the map provided:

yellow = Canada   orange = United States   red = Mexico
green = Central America   purple = Caribbean Islands

Now draw a brown line surrounding Middle America.

Regions of North America

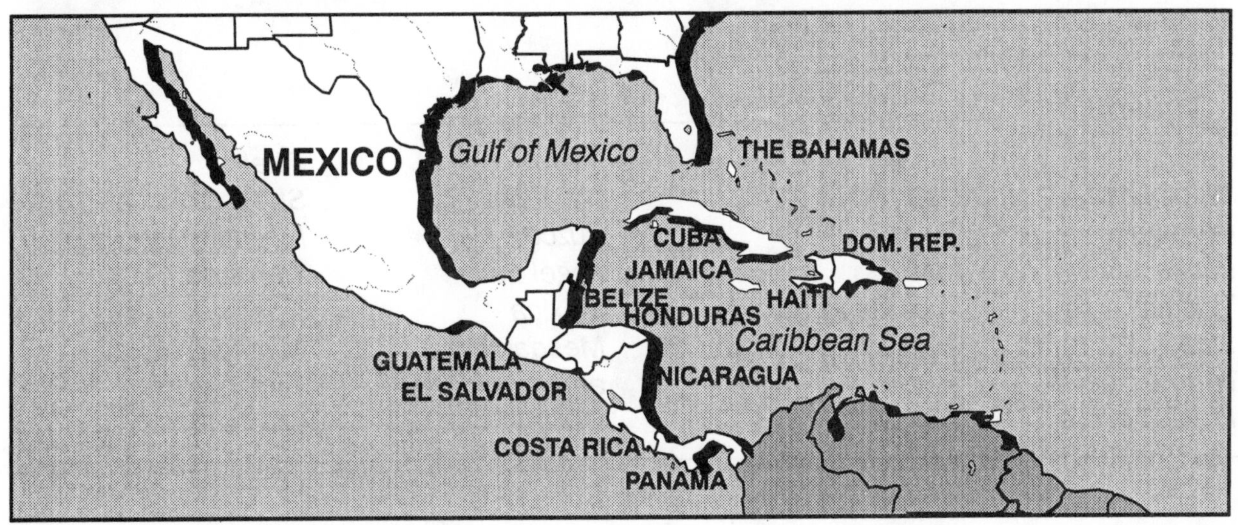

Latin America

Where Is Latin America?

Themes of Geography: *Location, Place, Region*

Objectives

Students will
1. use atlases and maps to identify historical locations
2. identify absolute location of historical Latin America
3. describe relative location of early Latin American civilizations
4. create a mental map of Pre-Columbian civilizations

Rationale

Historical geography is a study of the past in geographic terms, involving changes in the land and the people who lived on it. Humankind and the environment influence each other in many measurable ways. Modern geography tries to connect information about humans, time, and location to develop a pattern. The pattern can be used to understand the past, to read the present, or to predict the future.

The meshing of time and space can really be seen in the culture hearths of Middle America. Middle America is often confused with Central America and Latin America. This unit clarifies the position of Middle America in a historical geography context.

Skills Taught in This Unit

Map reading
- Absolute location
- Relative location
- Use of mental mapping

Analysis

Vocabulary

Tenochtitlán	*El Tajin*	*Maya*	*Tikal*
Tegucigalpa	*New World*	*Mt. Pelee*	*St.-Pierre*
Cartagen	*Quito*	*Cuzco*	*Machu Picchu*
Pachacuti	*Inca*	*Angel Falls*	*Tierra del Fuego*
Titicaca	*Yucatan Peninsula*	*Mexica*	*Aztec*
Inca	*Andes*	*Mesoamerica*	*Middle America*
culture hearth	*Toltec*	*anthropologists*	*Tarascan*
Pre-Columbian	*Arawak*	*Carib*	*altiplano*

Absolute Location in Latin America

Whether Pre-Columbian (before the arrival of Columbus in the Americas) or modern-day, unique examples of historical geography are documented in Mexico, Guatemala, Honduras, the Bahamas, the Dominican Republic, Martinique, Colombia, Ecuador, Peru, Chile, Bolivia, and Venezuela. Some of the most outstanding examples are offered in this lesson.

Materials: "Absolute Location in Latin America" activity sheet, pencils, atlas (or other reference books), paper, colored pencils (or markers or crayons), rulers, scissors, glue, construction paper of various colors, old magazines, wallpaper pattern books, tape recorder w/microphone, audio cassette tapes, video camera, video tapes

OPTIONAL: computer with desktop publishing/graphic/multimedia capabilities

Directions
Guide students' reading of the activity sheet. If not done previously, use the minute portions of the absolute location coordinates to reinforce just how specifically we can pinpoint locations on the earth. Use of degrees, minutes, and seconds for latitude and longitude are precise. Students use the creative means that best fits their learning style to invent the travel item of their choice.

Relative Location in Latin America

Early civilizations in Latin America do not include just the Aztecs, Incas, and Mayas. Several lesser-known civilizations also added remarkable contributions to world civilizations and history. Anthropologists studying the customs of primitive peoples have proven just how advanced many of the Latin American societies actually were.

To distinguish among Latin America, Middle America, and Central America, one must understand geography, history, and culture. *Mesoamerica* is the name most anthropologists give to the *culture hearth* or the place of origin of a major culture such as the Aztecs.

Materials: "Relative Location in Latin America" activity sheet, pencil, atlas (or other reference book), Western Hemisphere map, paper, colored pencils (or markers or crayons)

Directions
Brainstorm a list of early civilizations that were found throughout Latin America. Guide students' reading, descriptions, and mapping of the activity sheet. Use students' mental maps to review brainstorming. Distinguish between Latin America, Middle America, and Central America. Also, clarify whether Caribbean Islands are in the Greater Antilles or the Lesser Antilles.

Name ______________________

Absolute Location in Latin America

Latin America has a rich cultural heritage with many historical locations. Mexico City, (Mexico's capital), was called *Tenochtitlán* by the Aztecs. It was located on an island in a lake. Another historical Mexican location is the pyramids at *El Tajin,* northeast of Mexico City. The *Maya* temple-pyramid ruins of *Tikal* are located in Guatemala. Honduras is famous for its sixteenth century "silver hill," *Tegucigalpa.* Columbus first visited the New World on the Bahamas, and the first permanent English settlement in the *New World* was in the Dominican Republic. Martinique's *Mt. Pelee* destroyed the old capital, *St.-Pierre.* Colombia's 60-foot-thick stone walls at *Cartagen* provided pirate protection. South America's oldest capital is located at *Quito*, Ecuador, complete with beautiful Spanish architecture. The Inca's old capital is found at *Cuzco,* Peru. *Machu Picchu* remains as the fifteenth-century royal estate of *Pachacuti,* founder of the *Inca* Empire. The "Land of Fire," as Magellan called *Tierra del Fuego,* belongs to Chile.

Using an atlas, identify which location is found at these absolute location coordinates:

1. ______________ 17°S 78°32'W
2. ______________ 10°30'N 75°40'W
3. ______________ 13°36'S 71°52'W
4. ______________ 14°08'N 87°15'W
5. ______________ 14°49'N 61°10'W
6. ______________ 17°16'N 89°49'W
7. ______________ 19°N 70°45'W
8. ______________ 19°28'N 99°09'W
9. ______________ 26°15'N 76°W
10. ______________ 53°50'S 68°45'W

11. *Angel Falls* is the world's tallest waterfall, cascading 3,212 feet off Devil Mountain in the country of ________________ located at 6°N latitude and 63°W longitude.
12. Lake *Titicaca* is the world's highest navigable lake at 12,500 feet above sea level. It is shared by the nations ________________ and ________________ at 16°S latitude and 70°W longitude.

You are a travel agent. Design a travel poster or brochure, newspaper or magazine advertisement, bumper sticker, or radio or television commercial advertising one of these historical locations.

Relative Location in Latin America

Early civilizations in the Latin American region included the Indians of Mexico. The *Yucatan Peninsula* Mayas, and later the high plateau *Mexica*, called the *Aztecs* by the Spanish, were two of these groups of Indians. Indians were the first people to live in the Caribbean. The Mayas were also located in Central America as far south as Belize, Guatemala, and Honduras. Indians populated South America, with *Incas* found mainly in the *Andes* Mountains.

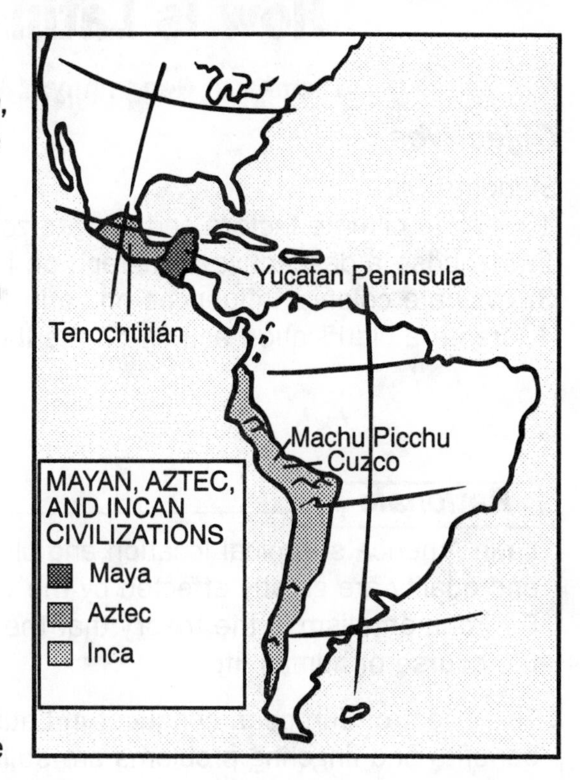

Mesoamerica is a name given to the *Middle American culture hearth* by *anthropologists*. The Mayan and Aztec locations in Mesoamerica are famous for their farming specialities, urbanization, transportation networks, architecture, art, religion, science, and writing achievements. *Toltec* and *Tarascan* civilizations also existed in Mexico's *Pre-Columbian* historical geography. The Toltec were in the Aztec high plateau of this plateau location. The Maya are often called the Lowland Civilization, while the Aztec are called the Highland civilization.

Arawaks were island Indians found on the larger islands (the Greater Antilles). The *Caribs* Indians populated the smaller islands (the Lesser Antilles). They were farmers and traveled over the water in huge canoes.

South America's Incas lived in the *altiplanos,* high in the Andes. The Incas were famous for their military victories and empire building. They used roads, bridges, and colonization.

On a separate sheet of paper, answer these questions.

1. Give the relative location(s) of each of the following:
   a. Arawaks
   b. Aztecs
   c. Caribs
   d. Incas
   e. Mayas
   f. Tarascans
   g. Toltecs
2. If we know that North America includes Canada and the United States and that South America is the continent below Panama, describe what locations are included in Middle America. Use an atlas or map of the Western Hemisphere to help you.
3. Design a mental map showing the early civilizations of Latin America.

How Is Latin America Unique?

Themes of Geography: *Location, Place, Interaction, Region*

Objectives

Students will

1. analyze climate factors and climate zones in Latin America
2. compose a descriptive paragraph on Latin American physical place characteristics
3. evaluate colonial influences on Latin American Indians
4. create a clarification activity on the Iberian influences in Latin America

Rationale

Latin America's tropical location and climate are important to agriculture. Crop diversity and quality are greatly affected by the varying degrees of elevation in the area. Environmentalism is the theory that the natural environment, to a great extent, dictates the course of human life.

The effect of European conquest in Latin America was a collision of cultures. Enduring benefits and lingering problems are still found in the transculturation among Spanish, Portuguese, and Latin Americans.

Skills Taught in This Unit

Map reading
Relative location
Analysis
Descriptive writing

Vocabulary

altitudinal zone
coca
paramos
Christopher Columbus
deforestation
Pedro Alvarez Cabral
relief
maize
Andes
Hernán Cortes
overgrazing
tierra calienta
tierra fria
tierra helada
hacienda
exploit
tierra templada
puna
Aconcagua
Iberian
urban

Physical Place Characteristics in Latin America

Nowhere else on the earth does altitudinal zonation impact a region as greatly as it does in the equatorial latitudes of Latin America. Usually only three climate zones are identified. There are five altitude zones in the highlands of Mexico, Guatemala, the Andes range from Colombia across Ecuador into Peru, western Bolivia, Argentina and Chile.

Materials: "Physical Place Characteristics in Latin America" activity sheet, paper, pencil

Directions
Discuss what *climate* is. Include the five major climate factors—latitude, altitude, winds and mountains, ocean currents, and proximity to water. Guide students' reading and analysis of the activity sheet. Descriptive writings may become diary or journal entries. Some could be presented as dramatic monologues or talk show interviews.

Human Place Characteristics in Latin America

The interaction between Spaniards and Latin Americans since the exploration era has impacted the human characteristics of this region more greatly than any other exchange. Some of the lasting remnants of colonization will be seen forever in Latin America. Acculturation also left many scars on this region that may be irreparable.

Materials: "Human Place Characteristics in Latin America" activity sheet, paper, pencil

Directions
Generate an introductory discussion on the age of discovery and exploration to determine students' perception of what Columbus discovered and which European nations had influences in the New World. Guide students' reading and completion of the activity sheet. Clarify any misconceptions students may have about the era of exploration. Print public notices on brown paper grocery bags, burning them around the edges. Create a eulogy or obituary as a gravestone rubbing, using paper roughened on a concrete surface with chalk or crayon.

Name ______________________________

Physical Place Characteristics in Latin America

Altitudinal zones are found in mainland Middle America and the western edge of South America. These are places with high *relief* and distinct local contrasts. Different local climates, soils, crops, domestic animals, and lifestyles are found at varying levels of altitude.

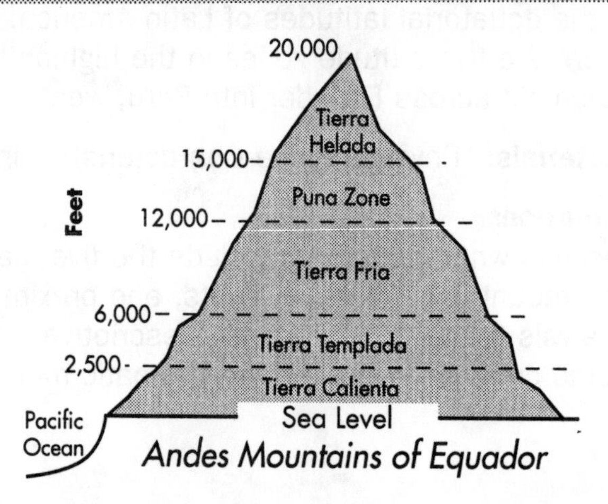

Andes Mountains of Equador

Tierra calienta (the "hot land") is the lowest, located from sea level to 2,500 feet. The coastal plains and low-lying interior basins are here. Tropical agriculture, growing bananas, cacao, rice, rubber, and sugar cane, flourishes in these places.

Tierra templada (the "temperate land") is the tropical highlands zone, extending up to about 6,000 feet. Mexico's Central Plateau and many Latin American highland plateaus and valleys are located in Tierra templada. *Coca*, coffee, cotton, *maize* (corn), potatoes, sugar cane, tobacco, wheat, and vegetables grow in this zone. This is also the most heavily populated place in Latin America.

Tierra fria (the "cold land") is the area of highest elevation. It extends from about 6,000 feet to nearly 12,000 feet. These highlands produce barley, beans, maize, oats, potatoes, and wheat. The timberline at 9,000 feet has the *puna* (also called the *paramos*) zone, from about 12,000 to 15,000 feet. Only hardy livestock and sheep or llama and alpaca grazing occurs here because it is so cold and barren. The highest zone is the *tierra helada* ("frozen land"), above 15,000 feet with permanent snow and ice. Mt. *Aconcagua* stands 22,831 feet above sea level in the *Andes* Mountains, the longest mountain chain in the world.

These ranges in altitude are used for comparing highlands lying in the equatorial latitudes. Latin America has better examples of these physical place characteristics than Africa or Asia.

1. What are the three climate zones found in Latin America? ______________________________, ______________________________, and ______________________________.
2. How do latitude and elevation affect climate? ______________________________
____
3. Why is it critical to understand the relationships among climate, elevation, and latitude?
____
4. If an acre of coca, the raw ingredient of cocaine, brings in $5,000 to $10,000 and an acre of corn $150 or so, why have many farmers taken to growing coca as a cash crop?
____

Imagine that you are moving from one Latin American climate zone to another. Describe how your life will change if you are an athlete training for the Olympics or a farmer seeking a better life for your family.

Human Place Characteristics in Latin America

Latin America has ties to Spanish heritage. but Brazil is more closely associated with Portuguese influences. *Christopher Columbus* arrived in the Indies in 1492, followed by *Hernán Cortes* in 1519. One reason the Spanish easily defeated the Aztec empire in 1521 was the superior Spanish weaponry (horses and artillery). Another reason was the mortal illness caused by diseases brought by the Spanish, diseases from which the Indians had no immunity. The Portuguese first settled in Brazil in 1532, led by *Pedro Alvarez Cabral.* Spain controlled Brazil from 1580-1640 because Spain had conquered Portugal.

A hacienda owned by a Spanish Colonist

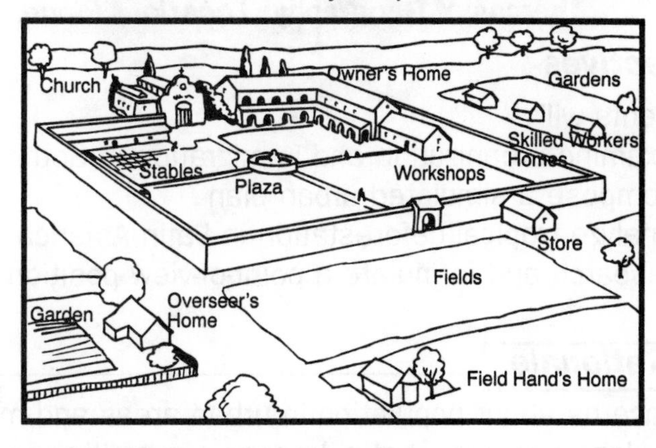

Conquests by the *Iberian* powers brought Spanish and Portuguese influences into Latin America. The Indians saw a drastic population decline, rapid *deforestation, overgrazing,* substitution of Spanish wheat for Indian *maize* on cropland, and construction of new Spanish towns using wood instead of stone. New languages, the dominance of the Roman Catholic religion, the layout of colonial towns in a grid-plan for administrative control, and diseases (influenza, measles, mumps, smallpox, and typhoid fever) were also brought by the Europeans into this region. Ultimately, the Spanish *exploited* the land's mineral wealth, especially gold, silver, and copper.

Indians were forced from traditional farming into towns and villages established by the Spanish. Often the new settlements were not suitable for farming. Food shortages and famine resulted, but the settlements were seldom abandoned. Each *urban* area was unified by the Catholic church, just as it is today. Giant *haciendas* emerged in South America when lands were taken from the Indians. Taxes were imposed and a forced-labor system was begun to get the maximum profits from this exploitation. Latin America was changed forever by the Iberian invasion.

The following activities should be done on a separate sheet of paper.

1. Design a time line showing 1400 to 1700 in Latin America, with events given in the correct order for the Portuguese and Spanish influences in this region.
2. Explain the negative effects the European conquerors had on the Indians of Latin America.
3. Describe the lasting influences the Iberian invasion had on Latin America.
4. Plan a public notice to be posted in a Latin American place concerning why the Spanish or Portuguese have a right to take a particular position in that community.

How Does Interaction Affect Latin America?

Themes of Geography: *Location, Place, Interaction, Movement, Region*

Objectives

Students will
1. examine urbanization and immigration in South America
2. compose a simulated urban plan
3. analyze tropical deforestation in Latin America
4. research and formulate a point-of-view position on rainforest deforestation

Rationale

Concerns about population in urban areas and migration from rural areas are growing in developing regions. Latin America exemplifies some of the most critical reasons for understanding the problems and consequences of urbanization.

The destruction of a biome and the endangering of animals, plants, and livelihoods is best exhibited in the earth's tropical rainforests. Nowhere else on earth are we finding a more graphic example of human impact than on this ecosystem. If dire predictions are true, only a few years remain before this once extensive habitat will barely exist.

Skills Taught in This Unit

Map reading   Analysis   Point-of-view writing   Research
Relative location

Vocabulary

urbanization	*rural*	*urban*	*migrate*
immigrant	*infrastructure*	*biologist*	*deforestation*
nutrient	*global warming*	*slash and burn*	*smelt*
greenhouse effect	*habitat*	*biome*	

Rural-to-Urban Migration

Urban planning, especially in Less Developed Countries (LDCs), is an ever-increasing problem. Many demographers who study population characteristics know that humans cannot continue to overpopulate the earth as has occurred in the last few centuries.

Migration from rural to urban areas in Latin America, mainly South America, is a grave issue. South America is already the location of three of the ten largest urban areas in the world. Demands and stresses placed on the cities come from many sources. Some are predictable and solvable, while others are spontaneous and difficult to detect and solve.

Materials: "Rural-to-Urban Migration" activity sheet, paper, pencil

Directions
Brainstorm how cities emerge and are designed. Lead a discussion about the use of a central business district, commercial and industrial areas, elite residential section(s), and poverty areas, ie., Latin America's *barrios* or *favelas.* (Be certain to define these terms.) Guide students' reading of the activity sheet. Offer further discussions using materials students have obtained through their research as they design their urban plans.

Deforestation

Deforestation of Latin America's tropical rainforests is a major environmental concern. The world derives many known (and probably many more unknown) benefits from this ecosystem. Humans are now realizing (almost too late) the severe stress various occupations and business endeavors place on this region.

Point-of-view writing should be distinguished from clarification writing. One's opinion should be substantiated with factual documentation in the point-of-view method. Viewpoints must be accepted as credible, but should also be supported with knowledgeable defenses.

Materials: world map giving rainforest areas, "Deforestation" activity sheet, paper, pencil, research materials/facilities on tropical rainforest deforestation (free materials are available from numerous organizations, ie., The Rainforest Alliance, The World Wildlife Foundation)

Directions
Using the world map showing rainforests (atlas, transparency), discuss where the world's remaining rainforests are located. Emphasize the largest location of rainforests in South America (and Africa). Guide students' reading of the activity sheet. Offer time and resources for the research. Point-of-view presentations can be done as a point-counterpoint dramatization.

Rural-to-Urban Migration

Urbanization is the process by which people move into cities and towns to live. In South America people are leaving *rural* areas to move into cities at a rate seen nowhere else in the developing world.

Date	Urban Dwellers in South America
1925	33 percent
1950	40 percent
1960	49 percent
1970	57 percent
1975	60 percent
1980	65 percent
1990	75 percent

Overall, the *urban* population of South America has grown annually by nearly 5 percent since 1950. The rural areas have increased by only about 1.5 percent annually.

Southern South America has the highest percentages of rural loss in the region. About 85 percent of the citizens of Argentina, Chile, and Uruguay live in cities and towns. Seventy-five percent of Brazilians live in urban areas. Three of the world's ten largest cities are São Paulo and Rio de Janeiro in Brazil, and Buenos Aires, Argentina.

People *migrate* into cities mainly because of poverty. They hope for a better life in urban areas—better education, housing, jobs, medical care, social status, and entertainment. Instead, people often find slums without basic necessities. Often, they are homeless, underemployed or unemployed, and at the mercy of unsanitary conditions and diseases. They have few or no educational opportunities and find even less entertainment and excitement. Upper and middle class areas exist next to areas of great poverty.

South America's urbanization exceeds Middle America's by 10 percent. It is also greater than other Third World regions in Africa and Asia. Urban geography will be a major force in twenty-first-century South America.

Suppose you are the mayor of an urban area of 18 million people somewhere in South America. World organizations have projected that your population will reach over 23 million by the year 2000. You must create an urban plan for the future. Take into account that there are approximately 40,000 *immigrants* coming into your city every month.

1. How will you provide for the following?
   a. Housing
   b. Jobs
   c. Education
   d. Medical care
   e. Water rights
   f. Crime prevention
   g. Cultural activities
   h. Maintaining/improving *infrastructure*
2. Consider the following:
   a. How will you involve the immigrant community in the planning?
   b. What role would you expect the national and state governments to play?
   c. What benefits do you think the immigrants will bring to your city?

Deforestation

Biologists say that the destruction of the tropical rainforest in Latin America is the world's fastest *deforestation*. Tropical deforestation began during the Spanish Colonial era. The rate of destruction has dramatically increased in recent years. Only six percent of the earth's land area is now covered by rainforests.

El Salvador has already lost its entire rainforest area. Six additional countries will reach complete deforestation by the twenty-first century. One of two large areas of rainforests predicted to remain in the twenty-first century will be in the western Amazon Basin of South America. The reasons and consequences for tropical deforestation vary.

Some of the reasons:

- Rural lands are cleared for pasture. Many nations, especially Costa Rica, want to become meat producers and exporters.
- Logging is done by the lumber industry. Worldwide demands for housing, paper, and furniture cause excessive logging.
- Increase in need for firewood and cropland due to an increasing population.
- Mining to fill the need for *smelt* iron, manganese, copper, and other mineral ores.

Some of the consequences:

- Because the soil is so *nutrient*-poor, the land becomes useless for pasture after just a few years of grazing. It is eventually abandoned, erodes, and floods.
- The *slash-and-burn* method of deforestation releases a huge amount of carbon dioxide into the air. The carbon dioxide forms a blanket of gas that prevents excess heat from escaping earth's atmosphere. The result is the *greenhouse effect*. This *global warming* leads to higher world temperatures, polar icecap melt, and a substantial rise of sea levels. Higher sea levels endanger earth's crowded coasts.
- Lives of Indians native to the rainforest are threatened when their hunting and gathering *habitat* is destroyed.

The rainforests are biologically the richest and most diverse areas on our planet. They contain over half of all animal and plant species. Valuable food, medicinal, and industrial products come from this *biome*.

Research this topic and present your point of view on how the rainforests can be saved while at the same time allowing farmers, ranchers, loggers, and miners to live and work in harmony with their environment. Consider how governments can develop compromises between opposing sides on this issue. Is it possible to halt and even reverse environmental trends like global warming? Can reforestation revive endangered species of plants and animals?

What Are the Latin American Regions?

Themes of Geography: *Location, Place, Interaction, Movement, Region*

Objectives

Students will

1. identify and locate regions within Latin America
2. differentiate places within Latin American subregions that are interpreted differently

Rationale

The people of Latin America do not refer to themselves as Latin Americans. They say they are Brazilian, Panamanian, Mexican, Haitian, etc. Individual identity by country, ethnic origin, and heritage are important to the people of Latin America.

The 33 countries that comprise Middle and South America do share the unifying characteristic of Latin-based languages, however. Conquered by the Spanish, Portuguese, and French, the Native Americans who survived learned to speak the languages of their conquerors. Those languages, Spanish, Portuguese, and French, are all based on Latin, the language of the ancient Roman conquerors of Spain, Portugal, and France.

Latin America is geographically divided into regions and subregions that better reflect individual countries' heritage, ethnicity, and national identity. Despite the introduction of European ideas, religion, and culture, Latin America is a unique place with unique people.

Skills Taught in This Unit

Map reading
- Relative location
- Use of color key/legend

Analysis

Vocabulary

Latin America	*Central America*
Middle America	*mainland*
Greater Antilles	*Lesser Antilles*
Windward	*Leeward*

Regions Within Latin America

Latin America, Central America, and Middle America are not synonyms. They are names geographers have given to regions subdivided into smaller sections. Latin America is the largest of the geographical areas, extending from the Rio Grande River and northern Mexico all the way south to Cape Horn on the tip of the South American continent. The Caribbean Sea islands of the Greater and Lesser Antilles are also included within Latin America.

Middle America is a subsection of Latin America that includes Mexico through the isthmus of Panama and the Caribbean Islands. Middle America does not include any portion of the continent of South America. Middle America is literally in the middle of the Americas, between North America and South America.

Central America includes only seven nations. No Caribbean Islands are included in Central America. Central America is a subregion of Middle America; Middle America is a subregion within Latin America.

Materials: "Regions Within Latin America" activity sheet, outline political map of Latin America (as large-scale as possible to include the Caribbean Islands), colored pencils (or markers or crayons)

Directions
Lead a discussion on national pride and ethnic heritage. Help generate a list of students' perceptions of the countries included in Latin America, Middle America, and Central America. Guide students' reading and mapping of the activity sheet. Review the list to update and correct students' perceptions of these three regional identities.

Regions Within Latin America

Latin America, Central America, and *Middle America* are often used interchangeably. Actually, these are quite distinctly different regions of this part of the Western Hemisphere.

Latin America derives its name from the Latin languages, mainly Spanish and Portuguese, spoken in this region. Latin America's land mass reaches from Mexico south through Middle and Central America to the southern tip of the continent of South America. It also includes the Caribbean Islands.

Middle America includes all the *mainland* and island countries and territories between the United States of America and the continent of South America—Mexico, the Greater Antilles (Cuba, Hispaniola with the Dominican Republic and Haiti, Jamaica, and Puerto Rico), the Lesser Antilles (Anguilla, Antigua and Barbuda, Bahamas, Barbados, Cayman, Dominica, Grenada, Guadeloupe, Martinique, Montserrat, the Netherlands Antilles: Aruba, Bonaire, Curaçao, Saba, St. Eustacius, St. Lucia, St. Vincent and the Grenadines, Trinidad and Tobago, Turks and Caicos, the British Virgin Islands, the United States Virgin Islands, St. Croix, St. John, St. Thomas), and the seven Central American nations, including Panama.

The Caribbean Islands are sometimes divided into the *Greater Antilles* (the largest islands) and the *Lesser Antilles* (the smallest islands). There are also some that are called the *Windward* (Dominica south through Trinidad and Tobago) and the *Leeward* (Virgin Islands south through Guadeloupe) among the Lesser Antilles.

Central America is literally found within Middle America. Central America includes the nations on the mainland of the Americas between Mexico and Panama—Belize, Costa Rica, El Salvador, Guatemala, Honduras, Nicaragua, and Panama (some geographers and Panamanians do not include Panama in Central America).

Use a map of Latin America, an atlas, and the information provided on this page to complete these activities:

1. Color the following regions: Mexico, blue; Central America, yellow; South America, orange; Greater Antilles, green; and Lesser Antilles, red. Draw a brown circle around Middle America.
2. Create an outline of Middle America. Include countries and islands.

Regions of Latin America

Commonwealth of Independent States

Where Is the CIS?

Themes of Geography: *Location, Place, Region*

Objectives

Students will
1. use atlases and maps to identify absolute location
2. create rebus puzzles representing absolute location
3. describe the relative location of Commonwealth of Independent States (CIS)

Rationale

A study of Europe and Asia should include some references to the 15 nations that made up the Union of Soviet Socialist Republics (USSR) prior to 1991. Eleven separate countries united as the Commonwealth of Independent States (CIS). Georgia initially joined the CIS in April 1991, but withdrew before the December 21, 1991, Alma-Ata agreement. The CIS came into existence at the same time the European Union was emerging in Maastricht.

Skills Taught in This Unit

Globe and map reading
- Absolute location
- Relative location

Analysis
Computation

Vocabulary

Mount Ararat	*Yerevan*	*Nagorno-Karabakh*	*Caspian Sea*
Minsk	*Silk Road*	*Mount Elbrus*	*Tallinn*
Orthodox	*Tbilisi*	*Joseph Stalin*	*Aral Sea*
Lake Ysyk-Kol	*Riga*	*medieval*	*Palanga*
St. Basil's Cathedral	*Lake Baikal*	*Pamirs*	*Chernobyl*
Kara Kum Canal	*Bukhoro*	*Samarquand*	*Toshkent*
Ukraine	*Siberia*	*Armenia*	*Azerbaijan*
Belarus	*Kazakhstan*	*Kyrgyzstan*	*Moldova*
Russia	*Tajikistan*	*Turkmenistan*	*Uzbekistan*
European Russia	*Asian Russia*	*Tropic of Cancer*	*Arctic Circle*
International Date Line			

Absolute Location in the CIS

The former Soviet Union, now called the Commonwealth of Independent States (CIS), is—and has always been—a vital and fascinating part of the world. Several locations in the CIS are particularly interesting and historically important. Some are political capitals, some are geographical features, some are tourist attractions, and some are areas of great economic importance.

Materials: "Absolute Location in the CIS" activity sheet, atlases, other reference books, pencils, paper (various weights and textures may be desired), paper clips (standard and jumbo size)

Directions

Guide students' reading of the information on the activity sheet. As the class discusses each location, point it out on a large map and mention its absolute location. Students will use their atlases to find the absolute location of the places listed on the activity sheet. Each student should select and create rebus puzzles using their names.

Rebus puzzles can strengthen the comfort level many develop for the more difficult pronunciations found in this region. Spelling is often not as significant as the attempt to identify a location that may have numerous names in the various languages spoken across the CIS. For many students, name recognition is best remembered by association.

Relative Location in the CIS

Eleven states are included in the CIS. Of the original 15 countries in the USSR, Estonia, Latvia, Lithuania, and Georgia all chose not to be a part of the CIS. The aim of the CIS is to coordinate intercommonwealth relations and to provide a mechanism for the orderly dissolution of the USSR. Since 1991, this has become a region of transition. Looking at the relative locations of these nations indicates that cooperation and stability are required for the CIS to endure. Serious challenges still face the commonwealth.

Materials: world map, "Relative Location in the CIS" activity sheet, atlas (or other reference books), pencils

Directions

While displaying the world map, define relative location and discuss with students the vastness of the CIS. Guide students' reading of the activity sheet and then have them answer the questions. When reviewing the activity sheet, have students point out on a map the various places mentioned on the activity sheet (tracing with a finger the longest coastline in the world, using the left-hand to note the sunrise of the Ukraine, using the right hand to note the sunset over eastern Siberia, and using an arm to indicate the CIS north of 35° north latitude).

Name ______________________

Absolute Location in the CIS

Many locations in the *Commonwealth of Independent States* are historically important.

- Russia is the largest country in the world. Also the largest country in the CIS, it crosses 11 time zones. Among its many historic locations, Russia is famous for *St. Basil's Cathedral* in Moscow, and *Lake Baikal,* the oldest and deepest lake in the world. The lake holds one fifth of the world's fresh water.
- Recent conflicts between Armenia and Azerbaijan in the *Nagorno-Karabakh* have made the news. *Mount Ararat,* near Armenia's capital of *Yerevan,* is where Noah's ark was said to have rested.
- *Joseph Stalin,* a tyrannical dictator who ruled (and terrorized) the USSR from 1929-1953, was from the country of Georgia. The leader of the Georgian *Orthodox* Church resides in *Tbilisi,* the capital of Georgia.
- Kazakhstan is Asia's fourth largest nation. It shares the *Aral Sea* with Uzbekistan. The cities of *Bukhoro, Samarquand,* and *Toshkent* in Uzbekistan are situated along the historic *Silk Road* that linked Europe to China.
- The headquarters of the CIS is located in *Minsk,* the capital of Belarus.
- Latvia's capital, *Riga,* is called "Paris of the Baltic" because of its *medieval* importance in culture and trade.
- Most of the world's valuable amber comes from *Palanga* in Lithuania.
- The world's largest irrigation and shipping canal, *Kara Kum Canal,* is located in Turkmenistan.
- *Ukraine* is famous for the 1986 nuclear disaster in *Chernobyl.*
- Moldova is important for its wine industry.
- Hot springs keep *Lake Ysyk-Kol,* one of the world's largest mountain lakes, unfrozen in Kyrgyzstan.
- Estonia's capital, *Tallinn,* hosts a huge dance and music festival every four years.
- Tajikistan's highest peaks, the *Pamirs,* are also Central Asia's highest peaks.

Using an atlas, identify the absolute location for each of the following:

1. Yerevan ______________
2. Tallinn ______________
3. Aral Sea ______________
4. Riga ______________
5. Moscow ______________
6. Pamirs ______________
7. Chernobyl ______________
8. Minsk ______________
9. Tbilisi ______________
10. Lake Ysyk-Kol ______________
11. Palanga ______________
12. Lake Baikal ______________
13. Kara Kum Canal ______________
14. Samarquand ______________

Design a rebus for two of these absolute locations. Syllables, sounds, pictures, single letters, sets of two or three letters, or punctuation marks are used to create a rebus. Place the absolute location on the reverse side of the rebus puzzle. Exchange your designs with a partner and decode each other's puzzles. **Moss** – *s* + [cow] = Moscow

Name ____________________

Relative Location in the CIS

The Commonwealth of Independent States extends almost halfway around the world. When the sun rises over *Ukraine,* it is setting over eastern *Siberia.* The longest coastline in the world is in the Commonwealth. This entire region is north of 35°N latitude. The chart below gives the land area (in square miles) and the size rank in the world for each of the 11 countries included in the Commonwealth of Independent States (CIS).

Country	Area (square miles)	Global Rank
Armenia	11,500	133
Azerbaijan	33,400	111
Belarus	80,200	84
Kazakhstan	1,049,200	9
Kyrgyzstan	75,642	85
Moldova	13,012	130
Russia	6,592,800	1
Tajikistan	55,300	93
Turkmenistan	188,417	51
Ukraine	233,100	43
Uzbekistan	172,700	55

Using an atlas and the information above, answer the following questions.

1. Which is the smallest of the nations in the CIS? ____________________
2. If *European Russia* is approximately 1,747,112 square miles, how much area does *Asian Russia* cover? ____________________
3. Which countries in the Commonwealth are among the world's ten largest? ________
4. Which CIS nation is closest to the *Tropic of Cancer*? ____________________
5. Which Commonwealth country is crossed by the *Arctic Circle*? ____________________
6. Which country in the Commonwealth is closest to the *International Date Line*? ____
7. Which countries in the CIS border the *Caspian Sea,* the lowest point in Europe? ____

   ____

   ____

8. Parts of Russia, Kazakhstan, Georgia, and Azerbaijan are European. Which CIS nations are completely Asian? ____________________

   ____

   ____

9. *Mount Elbrus* in Russia is the highest point in Europe at 18,510 feet above sea level. What mountain range contains this peak? ____________________

How Is the CIS Unique?

Themes of Geography: *Location, Place, Interaction, Region*

Objectives

Students will

1. scan ethnic diversity characteristics in the Commonwealth of Independent States
2. research ethnicity and other human place characteristics in the 11 states of the Commonwealth
3. investigate permafrost in Russia
4. compose a vignette about advantages and disadvantages of living in or visiting an area of Russia where permafrost exists

Rationale

To comprehend the challenges and conflicts that have arisen since the dissolution of the USSR, one must consider the vast ethnic diversity in the CIS. Strong nationalism is fragmenting areas of the commonwealth along ethnic lines. Irredentism (the desire to recover lands of which people have been deprived) is prevalent in the commonwealth. People strongly identify with others of their own ethnic group.

A vast portion of Russia is affected by permafrost of varying depths. The influence of permafrost on human activities is major. Mining, drilling for oil, agriculture, water, building, transportation, and disposal of wastes range from extremely difficult in the milder permafrost areas to impossible in the coldest areas.

Skills Taught in This Unit

Map reading
Analysis
Composition
Relative location

Vocabulary

permafrost	*bedrock*	*tundra*	*taiga*
humid continental climate	*Arctic Lowland*	*West Siberian Plain*	*bogs*
Central Siberian Plateau	*Yakutsk Basin*	*Eastern Highlands*	*Titular*
flora	*fauna*	*frost heaves*	*Persian*
ethnicity	*Slavic*	*Cyrillic*	Turkic

Physical Place Characteristics in Russia

Russia, the most northern and the largest of the Commonwealth states, has the misfortune of having the climatic characteristic called *permafrost*. With mighty rivers, coal and metal mines, oil and gas fields, lumber plants, industrial cities, and rail infrastructure, the Siberian, Eastern Frontier, Russian Core, and Far East regions hold the future for Russian economic development.

Materials: "Physical Place Characteristics in Russia" activity sheet, atlas (or other reference books) pencils, paper

Directions
Discuss Russia's position as the dominant state in the Commonwealth of Independent States. Review the location of the Arctic Circle in Russia and its various climates—tundra, taiga, humid continental, and steppe. Identify the nine physical regions within Russia—Russian Plain, Ural Mountains, Caspian-Aral Basin, West Siberian Plain, Central Siberian Plateau, Yakutsk Basin, Eastern Highlands, Central Asian Ranges, and Caucasus. Guide students' reading and examination of the map on the activity sheet. Small groups of students can identify the cities' permafrost depths to allow for interaction in this analysis. Then each student group can present a short vignette (similar to a brief scene in a play or movie) in which they present the advantages and disadvantages of living in—or visiting—one of the six Russian cities.

Human Place Characteristics in the CIS

Since 1991, the ethnic makeup of the Commonwealth has created political and cultural obstacles for many of these new states. From the Armenia-Azerbaijan conflict over Nagorno-Karabakh to strained relations between Kazakhstan and Uzbekistan, the isolation and poverty of Kyrgyzstan, and the Chechen separatists in Russia, it seems likely the ethnic alignment of the CIS is subject to change.

Materials: "Human Place Characteristics in the CIS" activity sheet, pencils, paper, several reference books

Directions
Guide students' reading on the activity sheet. Offer assistance as students do their research; make certain that they pay special attention to the ethnic makeup and diversity in the commonwealth states. Display the reports in the classroom, have students read their reports to the class, or have them exchange reports with partners and discuss what they have learned. Guide students as they form their groups and plan and make their presentations.

Name ____________________

Physical Place Characteristics in Russia

Permafrost is permanently frozen water in the soil and *bedrock*. The permafrost in Russia may be as deep as 300 meters (1,000 feet). It looks like frozen ground. However, permafrost thaws near the ground's surface during a brief warm season. The areas in Russia that contain permafrost are *tundra, taiga,* and the *humid continental climate* regions.

The *Arctic Lowland* extends from Finland to the East Siberian Sea. It is a continuous area of permafrost in Russia that reaches a depth of more than 500 meters. The *West Siberian Plain* has permafrost in the north and a marshy central area. The *Central Siberian Plateau* has a landlocked permafrost zone surrounded by continuous permafrost between 300 and 500 meters deep. The *Yakutsk Basin* and *Eastern Highlands* also contain vast expanses of permafrost between 100 and 500 meters deep.

Little economic activity takes place in Russia's northernmost tundra, the area north of the Arctic Circle. South of the tundra, in the taiga, the permafrost is less harsh. There, some forestry, some herding, and some hunting and gathering take place. Permafrost is a big challenge for Russia. Vast oil and mineral resources are located under the permafrost regions. Special technology is used in construction so that buildings and transportation systems like the Trans-Siberian Railroad and the Baikal-Amur Mainline (BAM) do not sink into the ground when the permafrost melts.

Permafrost Depth

A always more than 500 meters
B always from 300 to 500 meters
C always from 100 to 300 meters
D some up to 100 meters
E occasionally up to 25 meters

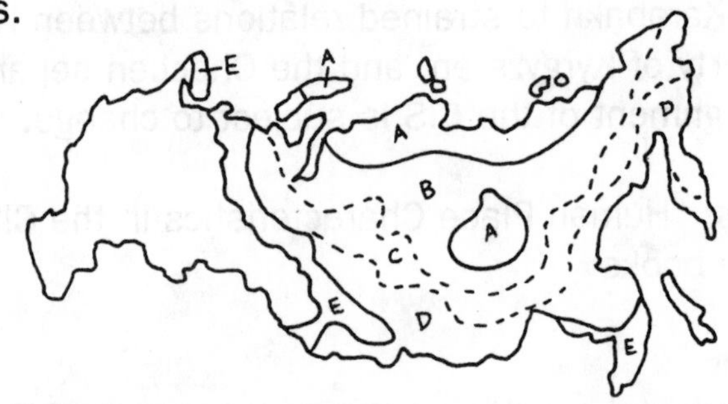

Using an atlas and this map, locate the following Russian cities and circle their permafrost depth.

1. Murmansk	A B C D E	2. Norilsk	A B C D E
3. Vladivostok	A B C D E	4. Magadan	A B C D E
5. Vorkuta	A B C D E	6. Bratsk	A B C D E

In your group, compose a short vignette portraying advantages and disadvantages of living in one of the six Russian cities you just located. Consider *flora, fauna,* natural resources, mineral deposits, *bogs* that hinder transportation, *frost heaves,* freezing of public utilities, infertile soils, very short growing seasons, and spring floods caused by snowmelt.

Name ____________________

Human Place Characteristics in the CIS

Variety is the key word in understanding the *ethnicity* of the Commonwealth of Independent States. The countries that form the CIS are divided mainly along ethnic lines. Some of these groups do not get along well with one another.

pree-VYET Hello	duh svee-DAHN-yuh Goodbye	DAH Yes	NYET No
puh-ZHAHL-stuh Thank you	spuh-SEE-buh Thank you		

Most of the people who live in Russia, Ukraine, and Belarus are *Slavic* and use the *Cyrillic* alphabet. About half of the population of the CIS are Russians. The Ukrainians live mainly in the southern part of the Commonwealth and are the second largest Slavic group. The Byelorussians live mainly in the western part of the CIS and are the third largest Slavic group. The Tartars are a *Turkic* group in European Russia. Some Russians belong to the *Titular* nationality.

The Armenians, the Azerbaijans, and the Georgians are the three major ethnic groups in the Caucasus. Armenia and Azerbaijan are the only states with populations that are less than eight percent Russian. The Kurds are one of more than 50 Caucasus ethnic groups.

The Muslim and Turkic-speaking people are the major ethnic group in Central Asia. Within this ethnic group, the Uzbeks are the most predominant people. Other factions are the Kazakhs, Kirghiz, and the Turkmen.

Tajiks also live in central Asia. However, they are not Turkic, but of *Persian* origin.

Kaliningrad, between Lithuania and Poland, was a German area prior to 1945. Many Germans were resettled there in 1990. Some ethnic groups, such as the Russian Jews and the German-speaking and the Polish-speaking people, do not have their own states.

1. Research one of the 11 states in the CIS and report your findings in a single page. Emphasize the human place characteristics of your state—its ethnic and religious makeup, its cultural heritage, and any political or economic struggles its people are experiencing.
2. In a group with a few of your classmates, do some studying (and maybe a little imagining) about the day-to-day lives of the people in one of the Commonwealth states. Consider their clothing, foods, jobs, religions, leisure activities, and anything else your group feels is important to make these people "come to life." Then make a presentation to the class about the people in your chosen country.

How Does Interaction Affect Russia and the CIS?

Themes of Geography: *Location, Place, Interaction, Movement, Region*

Objectives

Students will
1. examine rail transportation in Russia
2. compose a travel journal
3. analyze irrigation interactions in the Commonwealth of Independent States
4. recommend environmental solutions to save the Aral Sea

Rationale

Infrastructure is the most important requirement for modern transportation needs. Rail systems throughout the Commonwealth of Independent States are more developed than other transportation systems. Russia's Trans-Siberian Railroad is a twentieth-century reality that allows Russia access to the world, even with the harsh Siberian climates.

The condition of the Aral Sea is just one ecological problem humans have waited almost too long to solve. Many speculate that by the year 2010 the living standards in Kazakhstan and Uzbekistan will be reduced to the point that citizens will allow this sea to dry up completely.

Skills Taught in This Unit

Map reading Analysis Composition Computation Relative location

Vocabulary

Trans-Siberian Railroad	*Iron Ribbon*	*Chinese Eastern Railway*	*elevation*
inland sea	*surface area*	*irrigation*	*desertification*
defoliant	*pesticide*	*waterborne*	*reforestation*
Baikal-Amur Mainline	*salinity*		

Iron Ribbon

Asia, including Russia and the Commonwealth of Independent States, is very dependent on rail transportation. Goods, services, and people are more likely to be moved by railroads than by highways and air travel. Only water transportation, especially along rivers, rivals the rail systems in Asia's infrastructure.

The *Trans-Siberian Railroad* and the *Baikal-Amur Mainline* are Russia's pride. From Moscow to Vladivostok, passengers, minerals, and manufactured goods are carried over some of the world's vast barren landscapes by these parallel rail systems. Many Russian cities were built as the railroads were built.

Materials: "Iron Ribbon" activity sheet, pencils, paper

Directions
Discuss with students how transportation has changed since the Industrial Revolution and during the twentieth century. Guide students' reading of the activity sheet. Review with students the land and water forms, climate, points of interest, and lifestyles of Russia as journals are composed.

Aral Sea

Since the early 1960s, unprecedented environmental changes have taken place in and around this inland sea that some believe was once a part of the Mediterranean Sea. The amount of water in the sea and its surrounding aquifers is diminishing and has become more saline. The frost-free period around the Amu Darya Delta has decreased to less than 180 days. All of these factors affect cotton, the main cash crop, in this area. Health concerns related to drinking water and sanitation and respiratory ailments (including throat and lung cancer) have increased. Local fishing industries and cities dependent on these industries have vanished. Cropland, pastures, and fauna in the region have changed greatly. It is crucial to protect the Aral Sea and the standard of living which has grown from exports from this area. Some people feel that the region must diversify and rely less on irrigated agriculture.

Materials: "Aral Sea" activity sheet, pencils, OPTIONAL: calculators

Directions
Guide students' reading and answering of the activity sheet. Lead the discussion to help students see that numerous bodies of water are at risk. Use the following data to reinforce the concept of water as a nonrenewable resource.

How long a water molecule stays. . . .

Location	Residence Time	Location	Residence Time
atmosphere	9 days	oceans	120 years
rivers	2 weeks	seas and oceans	3,000 years
soil moisture	2 weeks-1 year	underground	as much as 10,000 years
large lakes	10 years	water at deepest point	up to 10,000 years
aquifers	hundreds of years	Antarctic ice cap	10,000 years

Name ____________________

Iron Ribbon

The *Trans-Siberian Railroad* is sometimes called the *Iron Ribbon.* It is the world's longest continuous rail line. From 1891 until 1916, Russia built this major transportation link in various sections across Siberia. Railroads are more vital in Russia than highways.

From Moscow to Chelyabinsk, then from Chelyabinsk to Novosibirsk, and from Vladivostok to Khabarovsk, construction was begun at both ends of the line. The Novosibirsk to Irkutsk sector (near Lake Baikal) was completed before the Transbaikal section from Lake Baikal to Sretensk. With the *Chinese Eastern Railway* in Manchuria and a short water connector across Lake Baikal, Russia completed this new transportation route across Asia in 1903. Later, the rail loop around the base of Lake Baikal and the section north of the Amur River were completed. Other Russian cities along this ribbon include Nizhny Novgorod, Perm, Yekaterinburg, Krasroyarsk, and Omsk. The Trans-Siberian crosses the Yablonovy Mountains at Chita in eastern Siberia near the border of Mongolia and Manchuria. It now totals 5,750 miles (9,250 kilometers) in length. Most passenger trains can travel the entire route in less than 11 days.

Since 1916, many branch lines have been added. Recently, much of the route has been electrified. From 1974 until 1984 a parallel rail line, the *Baikal-Amur Mainline* (BAM), was built north of the Trans-Siberian Railroad in eastern Siberia. It is 2,000 miles (3,200 kilometers) long.

The population of Siberia is concentrated in a narrow belt along the route of the Trans-Siberian Railroad. Russia's railroads total 54,000 miles in length and lead the world in freight service. Siberian Russia's railroad system, like much of Asia's, is much more developed than its road system. Many of Siberia's minerals are moved out of Russia via the Iron Ribbon.

Prepare a ten-day journal describing a passenger's travels from Moscow to Vladivostok (or traveling west from Vladivostok) on the Trans-Siberian Railroad. Be certain to describe the landscape, your fellow passengers, and your purpose for traveling.

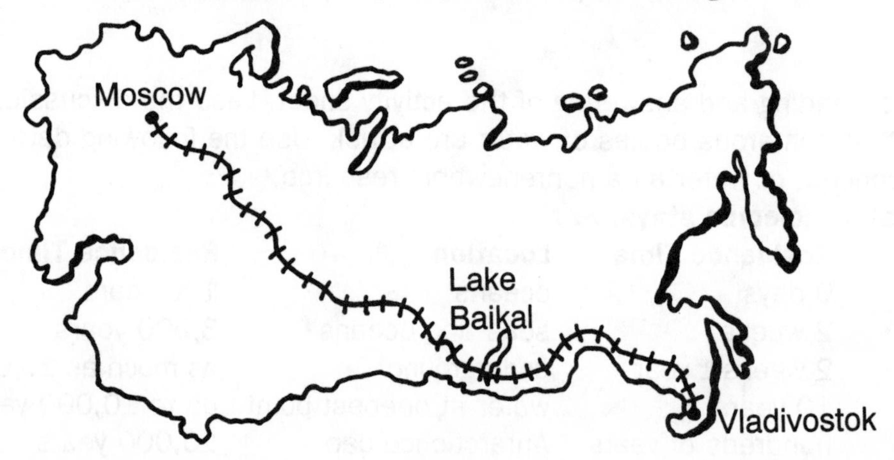

Name ______________________________

Aral Sea

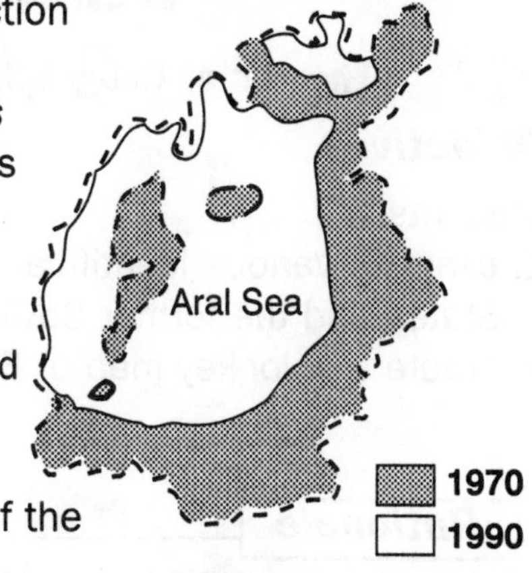

One of the grave consequences of inappropriate human interaction with the central Asian environment is apparent in the Aral Sea. Shared between Kazakhstan and Uzbekistan, this *inland sea is* disappearing. It has shrunk to one-third its original size and has lost more than 40 percent of its *surface area* since 1960.

The Amu Darya and the Syr Darya Rivers feed the Aral Sea. However, sixty percent of the water from these rivers is diverted before it reaches the Aral Sea. *Irrigation* for cotton, rice, and tobacco by the rapidly growing populations of Kazakhstan and Uzbekistan was originally the primary cause for the reduction of the water in the sea. Now the area suffers from *desertification;* contamination by fertilizers, *defoliants, pesticides;* and agricultural overproduction. Over 11,000 square miles of sea bottom are now a desert of sand and salt. The *salinity* of the remaining water has increased to the point that many native species have disappeared. As the coastline moves inland, many harbors and ports have become useless. Climate has become much more severe in Kazakhstan without the moderating effects of the Aral Sea. Diseases, especially *waterborne* diseases which cause 20 percent of the infant deaths in Uzbekistan, are a major concern.

This ecological disaster affects both climate and human health. Plans to restructure agricultural production, to plan for *reforestation,* and to improve public health do not include any measures to restore the Aral Sea's water supply. Many believe it will take decades to correct this situation. Some have suggested pumping Siberian water from the Ob and Irtysh Rivers to the Aral Sea along a new 1,600-mile irrigation canal.

1. There are 35 major seas in the world. Of these, eight—the Aral, Baltic, Bering, Black, Caspian, Mediterranean, South China, and Yellow—are called the "dying seas." Which of these are located near or in the Commonwealth of Independent States region?
   ____
2. The Aral Sea's surface *elevation* is 174 feet above sea level today. If it has dropped almost 9 feet (3 meters) since 1960, what was its elevation in 1960? ____________
3. If the Aral Sea covers 24,700 square miles today, and has lost about 40 percent of its area since 1960, how much area did the Aral Sea cover in 1960? ____________
4. The annual precipitation in the area around the Aral Sea is under 25 centimeters (10 inches) annually, similar to that of a middle latitude desert climate. What does this tell us? ______________________________

You are an environmental specialist. Do you agree with the proposal to pump water from Siberia to save the Aral Sea? What other solutions would you propose for Kazakhstan and Uzbekistan to save the Aral Sea? What can the other nations in the Commonwealth and the world do to help this situation? Write your proposals on another sheet of paper.

What Are the CIS Regions?

Themes of Geography: *Location, Place, Interaction, Movement, Region*

Objectives

Students will
1. examine various identifications for regions within the Commonwealth of Independent States and the former Soviet Union
2. create a color-key map of Eurasia

Rationale

The collapse of the Union of Soviet Socialist Republics in 1991 and the subsequent emergence of the Commonwealth of Independent States are two of the most significant political events in the twentieth century.

Eleven of the USSR's original 15 countries joined together to form the CIS. The eleven countries are Russia, Belarus, Ukraine, Moldova, Kazakhstan, Uzbekistan, Kyrgyzstan, Tajikistan, Turkmenistan, Armenia, and Azerbaijan. The CIS is divided into three regions—Russia, Central Asia, and Transcaucasia. Russia, the largest member of the Commonwealth, is a federation composed of 21 republics. The federation is divided into four subregions—Russian Core, Siberia, Eastern Frontier, and Far East.

Skills Taught in This Unit

- Map reading
  - Relative location
- Analysis

Vocabulary

Soviet Union	*Baltic states*	*Transcaucasia*
supranationalism	*Central Asia*	*Eurasia*
counties	*krays*	*municipalities*
oblasts	*oblystar*	*regions*
republics	*voblastsi*	

Regions Within Russia and the CIS

When this region changed from a union to commonwealth, many states in the region underwent identity crises. Between the December 8, 1991, meeting in Minsk, Belarus (with Russia, Ukraine, and Belarus attending), and the December 21, 1991, meeting in Alma-Ata, Kazakhstan (with Armenia, Azerbaijan, Belarus, Kazakhstan, Kyrgyzstan, Moldova, Russia, Tajikistan, Turkmenistan, Ukraine, and Uzbekistan signing the CIS treaty), the Commonwealth of Independent States was created. *Supranationalism* is a popular term describing this newest world region.

Three of the non-members are the Baltic states (Estonia, Latvia, and Lithuania), and another nonmember is Georgia. The Baltic states showed no initial interest in joining the CIS. Georgia did express some interest in the beginning but was not admitted initially because of an internal military conflict. These four countries will be included in this activity, however, as they are culturally and politically connected to the rest of the region.

Within Russia, the four main subregions are the Russian Core, Siberia, the Eastern Frontier, and the Far East. Russia is still the largest nation in the CIS and in the world.

Materials: world map or map of Eurasia; "Where Are Russia and the CIS?" activity sheet; blank, outline political maps of Eurasia; pencils; colored pencils (or markers or crayons). OPTIONAL: Russian and Armenian dictionary or contact with Russian and Armenian people (students at local universities, embassy personnel in Washington, D.C., or United Nations' personnel in New York City)

Directions

While displaying world or Eurasian map, brainstorm with students why Eurasia is often divided into Europe and Asia, which nations are found in both Europe and Asia, and why redrawing maps since 1990 has been so controversial. Guide students' reading, mapping, and answering of the activity sheet. To define political divisions within the CIS, some foreign language dictionaries or contacts may be necessary. Debrief by reexamining brainstorming questions.

Name ______________________

Regions Within Russia and the CIS

Great changes occurred in this region in the twentieth century. The Soviet empire that had existed since 1917 crumbled in 1991. The *Soviet Union* (USSR) broke up into 15 separate countries. The people of the *Baltic states* of Estonia, Latvia, and Lithuania decided in October 1991 not to join the Commonwealth of Independent States. The people of Georgia also chose not to join the commonwealth (after first saying in April 1991, that they would be a part of the commonwealth). By December 1991, the Soviet Union ceased to exist. Russia (or the Russian Federation) is the largest of the nations in the commonwealth. Others include Armenia, Azerbaijan, Belarus, Kazakhstan, Kyrgyzstan, Moldova, Tajikistan, Turkmenistan, Ukraine, and Uzbekistan. *Supranationalism*, which means "of or involving a number of nations," is a popular term used in describing this region.

Russia's location places it in both Europe and Asia. The Ural Mountains divide it into European Russia and Asian Russia. Belarus, Estonia, Latvia, Lithuania, Moldova, and Ukraine are European nations. Armenia, Azerbaijan, Georgia, Kazakhstan, Kyrgyzstan, Tajikistan, Turkmenistan, and Uzbekistan are Asian nations.

Geographers often refer to Georgia, Armenia, and Azerbaijan as the *Transcaucasia.* Another unique realm within the CIS is *Central Asia.* This includes Kazakhstan, Uzbekistan, Turkmenistan, Tajikistan, and Kyrgyzstan. Often, these five nations are referred to as Muslim Central Asia. These are all Asian countries.

Within each of these states are found numerous *counties, krays, municipalities, oblasts, oblystar, regions, republics, and voblastsi.* Russia alone has 21 republics, 49 oblasts, and 6 krays.

Using a *Eurasian* map, color the following regions within the Commonwealth of Independent States:

Russia: green | Transcaucasia (except Georgia): yellow
Central Asia: orange | Other states in the CIS: blue

1. Which states from the former Soviet Union should not be colored as belonging in the Commonwealth of Independent States? ______________________
2. Draw a brown line across Russia, Kazakhstan, Georgia, and Azerbaijan to show which portions are European and which are Asian.
3. Which three Commonwealth states are located entirely in Europe? ______________

____

Regions of the Commonwealth of Independent States

Oceania (The Pacific Region)

Where Is Oceania?

Themes of Geography: *Location, Place, Region*

Objectives

Students will
1. identify places in Oceania when given absolute location coordinates
2. determine dates given in an international date line scenario
3. examine the volcanoes in the Ring of Fire
4. assess the relative location of Oceanic volcanoes

Rationale

The Pacific Ocean covers one third of the earth. It touches every continent except Africa and Europe. It extends almost halfway around the world. If all the earth's land areas were consolidated, they could fit into Oceania.

The region of Oceania is the largest of all geographic regions in total area and the smallest in land area. Because of Oceania's many volcanoes, it is also a very transitional area.

Skills Taught in This Unit

Globe and map reading	Analysis	Computation
Absolute location		
Relative location		

Vocabulary

Oceania	*continental island*	*coral*	*limestone*
volcanic	*archipelago*	*trench*	*reefs*
high islands	*low islands*	*trust territory*	*International Date Line*
Ring of Fire	*volcano*	*tectonic plate*	*arcs*
active volcanoes	*Antarctic Circle*	*atolls*	

Absolute Location in Oceania

The four regions within Oceania are Australia, Melanesia, Micronesia, and Polynesia. This water world in the Pacific Ocean extends from approximately 28° N latitude at Midway Islands to 46° 50'S latitude on New Zealand's South Island. In terms of longitude, Oceania extends from approximately 131°E at Palau to Easter Island at 109° W.

There are many unique locations and geographic features in this region, but some locations cannot be found on many globes and maps. Large-scale maps of Oceania are not readily available or used in many classrooms.

Materials: "Absolute Location in Oceania" activity sheet, pencils, atlases (or other reference books), globe. OPTIONAL: large-scale screen map of the Pacific Ocean

Directions

Display a globe (or large-scale map of the Pacific Ocean) while introducing Oceania to students. Discuss the vastness of Oceania and its minuscule islands. Guide students' reading of the activity sheet. After reviewing the activity sheet, discuss with students why the international date line zig-zags through Oceania so that political entities are on the same calendar dates.

Relative Location in Oceania

The Ring of Fire encircles Oceania. Nearly 75 percent of the world's approximately 850 known volcanoes are within the Ring of Fire. Many active volcanoes are formed on the Pacific Ocean floor and appear above sea level as islands. Volcanoes usually form along boundaries where one tectonic plate plunges beneath another (called subduction). The rocky slab melts as it dives down into the mantle (the layer of rock between the earth's crust and core). When the magma (hot melted rock), ash, gases, and other material from the magma chamber rise through a conduit, they erupt through the volcano's opening. Magma is called *lava* when it reaches the air. A volcanic hill or mountain is made of lava and other materials that come out of the opening and then cool and harden. The top of a volcano often has a large opening called a *crater*. A *caldera* is a broad, craterlike basin of a volcano that contains water. It is formed by a volcanic explosion or by the collapse of a volcano's cone. Volcanic belts such as the Ring of Fire develop where molten material from inside the earth erupts through the crust.

Materials: "Relative Location in Oceania" activity sheet, pencils, calculators

Directions

Guide students' reading of the activity sheet. Bring to students' attention that the active, Ring of Fire volcanoes are listed according to elevation above sea level. Also discuss that sometimes several of these volcanoes are not located on maps of Oceania. The dates of the latest eruptions may include the eruption of new or old fragmented material, the escape of liquid lava, or both. Active volcanoes exhibit a wide range of activity.

Name ____________________

Absolute Location in Oceania

Oceania is the water world of the Pacific Ocean. Many islands are found in Oceania. Australia is the largest, a *continental island.* From the Midway Islands south to the Auckland Islands, Polynesia, Melanesia, and Micronesia dot the ocean with more than 25,000 islands. These islands are made of *coral, limestone,* or *volcanic* material.

Archipelagoes and twenty-one seas are located within Oceania. *Atolls* and *reefs* are scattered throughout the world's deepest ocean. The Mariana *Trench* contains Challenger Deep, which is the deepest part (35,810 feet below the surface) at nearly seven miles beneath the Pacific's surface. Near the equator, Oceania extends more than 11,000 miles around the world, from Palau in the Philippine Sea to Easter Island in the southeast Pacific.

Volcanic *high islands* and coral *low islands* are terms used to categorize many Oceania locations. High islands include Guam (Micronesia's largest island that belongs to the United States as a *trust territory),* New Zealand (two islands that have the geographic diversity of an entire continent), Tahiti (French Polynesia's Society Islands in the Tuamotu Archipelago), and Hawaii (with Mt. Waialeale, the world's rainiest place). Low islands include the Marshall Islands with Bikini and Enewetak (known for their nuclear testing sites) and Kwajalein (the world's largest atoll). Kiribati (straddles the equator and *International Date Line),* Tuvalu (the capital is Funafuti, where an air traveler's luggage is tagged with FUN), and Papua New Guinea (which contains one of the world's largest swamps) also are low islands.

Using an atlas and globe, identify the place names of these absolute locations.

1. 1°30'S 173°E ________
2. 7°S 142° 15'E ________
3. 10°N 165°E ________
4. 14°N 143°20'E ________
5. 21°33'N 158°08'W ________
6. 26°50'S 109°W ________
7. 42°S 175°E ________
8. 5°20'S 174°E ________
9. 7°15'N 134°30'E ________
10. 12°N 144°E ________
11. 17°30'S 149°30'W ________
12. 25°S 135° E ________
13. 28°N 179°W ________
14. 50°30'S 166°30'E ________
15. The international date line is an imaginary line that marks the boundary between one day and the next. Going west across this line adds a day, traveling east subtracts one day. If you are in Nauru on a Tuesday and travel to Pago Pago in American Samoa for a soccer match that evening, what day of the week is it in Pago Pago?____________

Name ______________________

Relative Location in Oceania

The *Ring of Fire* is a narrow band of active *volcanoes* around three sides of the Pacific *tectonic plate.* It is located on the boundaries between the Pacific plates and bordering plates. Bordering plates include continental plates and smaller ocean plates. It circles Oceania from Alaska's Aleutian Islands through Kamchatka southwest through the Kuril Islands and Japan. Here the Ring of Fire splits and encompasses the Ryukyu and Bonin islands before it comes together again in the Philippines. From here, it travels easterly in a series of *arcs to* Tonga and south to New Zealand. The Ring of Fire then zig-zags across the Pacific Ocean and the Nazca Plate to the Andes in South America. It travels north from Chile through central Mexico and into the Cascades of the United States and northwest back to the Aleutians.

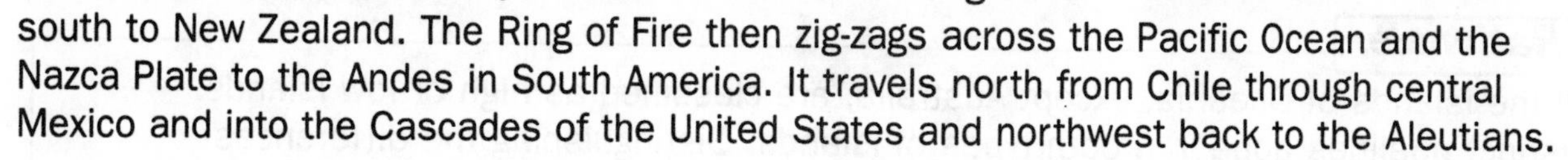

There are volcanoes on the bottom of the ocean and on every continent. About 850 *active volcanoes* exist in the world. Some have erupted many times. The Hawaiian Islands developed when volcanoes erupted under the Pacific Ocean. These are some of the notable active volcanoes in Oceania's Ring of Fire:

Name	**Location**	**Height (feet)**	**Latest Eruption**
Mauna Loa	Hawaii	13,680	1984
Ruapehu	New Zealand	9,175	1995
Ulawun	Papua New Guinea	7,532	1993
Bagana	Papua New Guinea	6,558	1993
Manam	Papua New Guinea	6,000	1995
Lopevi	Vanuatu	4,755	1982
Ambrym	Vanuatu	4,376	1991
Kilauea	Hawaii	4,090	1995
Langila	Papua New Guinea	3,586	1995
Rabaul	Papua New Guinea	2,257	1995
Pagan	Northern Mariana Islands	1,870	1993
White Island	New Zealand	1,075	1994

1. Which volcano in the Ring of Fire is closest to your home? ______________

Which of the locations with volcanoes . . .

2. is closest to Australia in Oceania? ______________

3. is closest to the *Antarctic Circle?* ______________

4. is closest to the international date line? ______________

5. has had the most eruptions? ______________

6. has a volcano with a height closest to one mile? ______________

How Is Oceania Unique?

Themes of Geography: *Location, Place, Interaction, Region*

Objectives

Students will
1. examine characteristics of high and low islands
2. study migration, diffusionism, and isolationism
3. research and cite examples of "push" and "pull" factors of human movement

Rationale

All the islands of Oceania, except Australia, are classified as high or low islands. Distinct qualities appear in both types of islands. Distinguishing the differences between these two types leads students into an analysis of several aspects of Oceania.

There are many theories about the movement of people and cultures throughout the world. Isolationists and diffusionists agree that there are many, some even remarkable, similarities between the Oceanic civilizations and those of the Americas, Asia, and the Mediterranean world.

Skills Taught in This Unit

Map reading
Relative location
Analysis
Research

Vocabulary

Oceania	*volcanic mountain*	*rainfall*	*winds*
forest	*refugee*	*coral reef*	*atoll*
lagoon	*aborigine*	*water*	*guano*
fishing	*coconut*	*subsistence*	*flora*
fauna	*diffusionism*	*migration*	*forced migration*
penal colony	*internal migration*	*push factor*	*pull factor*
isolationism	*voluntary migration*	*International migration*	

Physical Place Characteristics in Oceania

The soil of low islands is made of wind- and wave-eroded coral. It is thin and low in fertility, supporting minimal vegetation. Rainfall is scarce. For the most part, inhabitants eke out a subsistence living.

A high island has a greater elevation than a low island, usually because high islands are mountainous. Many high islands are peaks of mountains that are based on the ocean floor. There are many more advantages to living on the Pacific's high islands than on the low ones.

Materials: "Physical Place Characteristics in Oceania" activity sheet, pencils

Directions
Brainstorm with students why islands in Oceania are categorized as being either low or high. Guide students' reading of the activity sheet. Note that the total number of letters in the italicized words and the clue letters will help them decode the vocabulary assignment and ultimately the main physical features at the bottom of the sheet. Brainstorm again with students what distinguishes high from low islands.

Human Place Characteristics in Oceania

Diffusionism and isolationism are theories about how cultures spread. Archeologists and anthropologists have studied these theories for centuries. The relationships among various regions in the world, the steady movement of people, ideas, and cultures, and why cultural evolution brought us to where we are today are just some of the ideas to be considered.

Human migration provides an excellent example of the push and pull factors that bring about movement. This two-way action shows why movement is continuous.

Materials: "Human Place Characteristics in Oceania" activity sheet, pencils, dictionary or thesaurus, research materials (reference books: encyclopedias, almanacs, historical books and magazines; software: reference, database)

Directions
Guide students' reading of the activity sheet. *Intervening opportunity* (the presence of a nearer opportunity that diminishes the attractiveness of sites farther away) and *cultural diffusion* (the spread of a cultural element from its place of origin across a wider area) should be stressed with the research and discussion seminar.

Name ____________________

Physical Place Characteristics in Oceania

Read the following passage. Use the italicized vocabulary words to fill in the blanks on the right side. Use the numbered letters to fill in the blanks at the bottom of the page.

The high islands of *Oceania* are mainly *volcanic mountain* peaks. *Rainfall* is adequate on these islands because the mountains catch the *winds.* With the rich volcanic soil and abundant moisture, plants and crops grow well. *Forest* landscapes provide building materials for boats and houses. Many high islands also have valuable mineral resources. Because of their larger size and varied resources, these islands can support greater human populations and provide a better standard of living for their people.

The low islands of Oceania are characterized as being mainly *coral reefs* or *atolls* surrounding *lagoons.* Coral polyps, tiny sea creatures, build reefs with their hard outer skeletons. An atoll is a reef built around a volcano by innumerable coral. Over time, the volcano wears away or sinks beneath the *water,* while the reef continues to grow. Finally, the reef breaks through the surface of the water, forming a ring-shaped atoll or chain of islets (very small islands). Because these islands are so hard-surfaced, the rainfall they receive often runs off. Many islands suffer *droughts* because they do not have the mountains to catch the moisture-laden winds. The little soil they have is thin and sandy and is often broken and washed away by wind and waves. Drinking water is often scarce. *Guano,* bird droppings used as phosphate fertilizer, is the most valuable low island resource besides *fishing* and some agricultural products such as root crops and fruits, mainly *coconut.* Widely scattered groups of people live on these islands, but they live mostly a *subsistence* existence. There are some commercial plantations producing coffee, pineapples, and sugar cane. *Flora* and *fauna* in Oceania are dependent on how far the island is from its Asian source. Isolated islands have no mammals except the bat, no amphibians or reptiles except the sea turtle, and hardly any land birds. Remoteness has also preserved some ancient species (black pearls, Australia's marsupials, and the bird of paradise).

C _ _ _ _ _ (1)

F _ _ _ _ _ (2)

_ _ _ _ _ A (3)

_ U _ _ _ _ (4)

_ _ _ _ F _ (5)

_ _ _ I _ _ (6)

W _ _ _ _ _ (7)

_ I _ _ _ _ _ (8)

_ _ _ _ _ _ T (9)

_ _ _ _ _ _ U _ (10, 11)

_ I _ _ _ _ _ _ (12)

_ A _ _ _ _ _ _ (13)

_ _ _ _ A _ _ _ (14)

_ _ _ O _ _ _ _ _ (15, 16)

_ _ _ _ _ I _ _ _ (17)

_ _ _ _ N _ _ _ _ (18)

_ _ _ L _ _ _ _ _ (19)

_ _ _ _ S _ _ _ _ _ _ _ (20, 21)

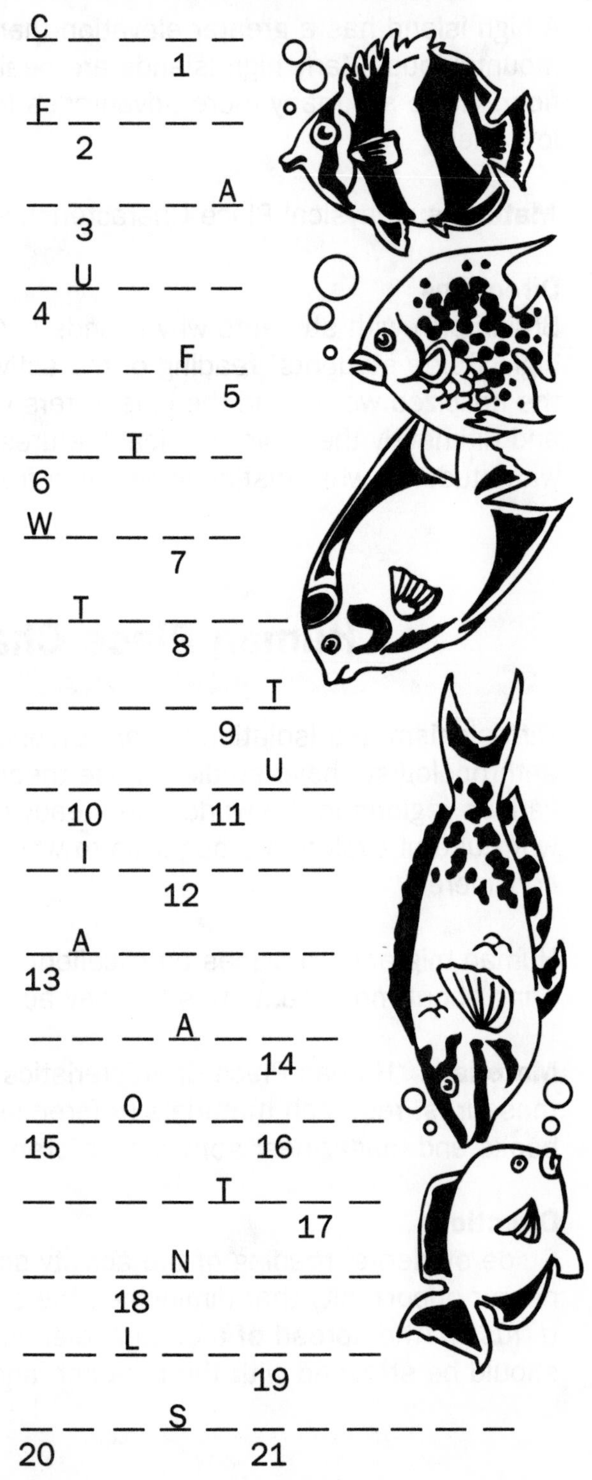

_ _ _ _ (12 14 4 16) _ _ _ _ _ _ _ (18 21 8 1 19 15 5) _ _ _ (3 10 6) _ _ _ _ _ _ _ (17 9 13 2 11 7 20)

Name ______________________________

Human Place Characteristics in Oceania

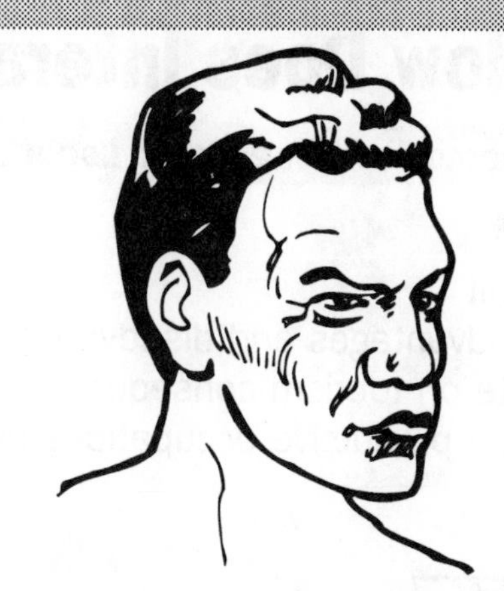

Diffusionism is one theory on how cultures spread in the Pacific. *Migration* is one type of diffusionism. There are four forms of migration—forced, internal, international, and voluntary. *Forced migration* occurs when people have no choice but to relocate. Prime examples are Australia's *penal colony,* established for British convicts; the *aborigines* who were forced into the Australian bush when Europeans arrived; and islanders who were forced to flee the Bikini and Enewetak atolls in the Marshall Islands after nuclear testing during World War II. (Bikini is still too radioactive today for habitation.)

Internal migration is the flow of people within a region. Island-hopping across land bridges and using boats to skim across the Pacific waters were two ways people in Oceania migrated and continue today to migrate from Asia. Some geographers feel that the people of Papua New Guinea are closely related to Australian aborigines, because of internal migration. The Maoris of New Zealand migrated from the Polynesian islands in this manner.

International migration is the movement of people across international boundaries. This is apparent in Polynesia. The Neo-Hawaiians are an ethnic blend of the original Polynesian, European, and Asian ancestors. International migration also accounts for the *refugees* from Indochina who have settled in Australia in recent years.

Voluntary migration is the relocation of people who are hoping for a chance to have a better life. Traditionally, the natives of these islands have moved freely, hunting, gathering, and fishing. Many Europeans came to Oceania seeking adventure, land, and work.

The theory of *isolationism* explains why some people and cultures have remained separate, kept apart from other people and places. For example, an ocean is often an effective barrier to human migration.

1. Define *migration.* ______________________________

2. List four types of migration. ______________________________

3. On the back of this sheet, explain the difference between *diffusionism* and *isolationism.*

4. Research various locations in Oceania for examples of forced, internal, international, and voluntary migration patterns. Describe these in a discussion with other members of your class on the *push* and *pull factors* that influence human movement.

How Does Interaction Affect Oceania?

Themes of Geography: *Location, Place, Interaction, Movement, Region*

Objectives

Students will
1. specify advantages and disadvantages of transportation in Oceania
2. speculate on tourism consequences for Oceania
3. categorize productive occupations of economic geography

Rationale

Oceania's infrastructure is affected by the environment. Some of the landforms that charm tourists also make it difficult to travel on the islands. Therefore, the region has reached many compromises with its infrastructure to maximize its attractions and to minimize inconvenience to industry.

Economic geography is sometimes called *spatial economics.* The geography of development and modernization is another name for this study. This subfield of geography is concerned with the different ways people can earn a living and how the goods and services they produce to earn that living are organized and distributed.

Skills Taught in This Unit

Map reading
Analysis
Relative location

Vocabulary

fossicking	*inter-island*	*intra-island*	*catamaran*
outrigger canoe	*schooner*	*ketch*	*infrastructure*
primary	*secondary*	*tertiary*	*quaternary*
gauge			

Transportation in Oceania

A study of transportation in Oceania allows students to examine traditional and modern modes of movement. The Pacific region is a good place in which to study travel. Barriers to movement can include national laws and the lack of knowledge of other places, people, cultures, and physical features. Technology has opened Oceania to modern travel. The tourism industry has become a viable hope for Oceania's future.

Materials: "Transportation in Oceania" activity sheet, pencils, physical-political map of Australia-New Zealand

Directions
Define *infrastructure* with students. Explain to them that this is a relatively new term coined during the twentieth century, as the relationship of humans with their world has grown and changed. Guide students' reading and answering of the activity sheet. Discuss other contemporary transportation terms that are new to this century (*propeller, turbojet, supersonic, helicopter, hovercraft, windshield wipers, rocket engine,* and *space shuttle*).

Economic Activities in Oceania

Oceania is typical among global regions in its economic progress. The economy has moved from sole dependence on agriculture to industry, service occupations, and management. Economically speaking, it is moving from the past and preparing for the future.

Materials: "Economic Activities in Oceania" activity sheet, pencils, four sheets of chart paper, markers

Directions
Display four sheets of chart paper, one each entitled "primary," "secondary," "tertiary," and "quaternary." Brainstorm the definitions of each of these terms with students, focusing on the prefixes as clues. Guide students' reading of the activity sheet. Have several students list the jobs of Oceania on the corresponding sheet of chart paper. Ask students to suggest additional occupations (and justify the categories in which they are placed). Ask what could become the fifth productive activity in the twenty-first century. What might it be named?

Name ____________________

Transportation in Oceania

Movement in the Pacific region has increased rapidly since the mid-1900s. People travel around the coasts and along the rivers by boat or by airplane.

Mountains make transportation and travel difficult on many Pacific islands. Dense rain forests and natural forces, such as typhoons, earthquakes, and landslides, often hinder the construction and maintenance of roads and railways. Australia has several deserts that hinder land travel. Water and air travel are the most reliable forms of transportation on the Pacific islands.

Helicopters and airplanes are common modes of transportation for many Pacific islanders. Papua New Guinea has over 425 airstrips. Some are located in very unlikely places—at the end of a cliff, on steep slopes, and in tiny clearings in the rain forest. Many people who have never seen a bus or train, or even a bicycle, regard the airplane as the common way to travel. *Fossicking* (searching for minerals) is often conducted by helicopter. Medical care is provided by air transport as well as by land.

Water transportation is also the norm in Oceania. Many people prefer a water route, even when a road is available. From fleets of large ships to small crafts, *inter-island* and *intra-island* movement of people and cargo provides income for individuals and revenue for nations. *Catamarans, outrigger canoes,* houseboats, ferries, water taxis, *schooners,* and *ketches* are some of the popular water vessels used by island inhabitants.

More-developed areas in Oceania tend to provide land *infrastructure* for their citizens. Towns are linked by roads on individual islands throughout Oceania. Most are not super highways of concrete or asphalt, however. Some roads require four-wheel-drive vehicles because of the mountains, sharp bends, steep ravines, and bridges which are sometimes submerged by swiftly flowing rivers. Very few connecting bridges and highways exist between the island nations scattered across Oceania. Australia now has more automobiles per capita and more road miles per person than the United States. Australia also had *gauge* railroads until 1970, when it coordinated its rail system from Sydney to Perth. Isolation is still a problem for parts of Oceania.

Answer these questions on the back of this sheet.

1. Describe some advantages for moving people, goods, and services by water in Oceania.
2. Examine a physical-political map of Australia and New Zealand. Identify examples of physical barriers to movement in Australia and New Zealand.
3. How has transportation technology influenced the rates at which people and goods move from place to place?
4. Speculate on the consequences to Oceania if all tourism were to cease.

Name ____________________

Economic Activities in Oceania

There are four basic types of activities in which humans participate that produce jobs. These are *primary, secondary, tertiary,* and *quaternary* activities. Each tells us how people interact and how they adapt to or modify the environment in which they live and work.

Primary activities are those in which workers and the environment come into direct, active contact. Agriculture and mining are examples of this type of economic activity.

Secondary activities are those in which workers take raw materials and produce something as a finished product. Manufacturing is a good example of this type of activity.

Tertiary activities are the wide range of jobs promoting, distributing, selling, or using what is made from raw materials. Service occupations—education, finance, retailing, and office work—would be involved in tertiary economics.

Quaternary activities are those responsible for collecting, processing, and manipulating information. This is the fastest-growing sector of most economies, even in Oceania. Jobs that deal with decision making in large organizations, such as managing and controlling businesses, are examples of quaternary activities.

At different times in history, each of these basic economic activities has been the primary one in most nations. An easy method of understanding these productive activities and how they show relationships is to categorize examples of them.

Analyze these job titles. Circle the letter of the type of activity that best describes each job.

P = primary S = secondary T = tertiary Q = quaternary

P S T Q 1. fisherman
P S T Q 2. logger
P S T Q 3. stockbroker
P S T Q 4. farmer
P S T Q 5. judge
P S T Q 6. soldier
P S T Q 7. hunter
P S T Q 8. cannery worker
P S T Q 9. engineer
P S T Q 10. oil driller
P S T Q 11. priest
P S T Q 12. tourism minister
P S T Q 13. rancher
P S T Q 14. pearl diver

What Are the Regions of Oceania?

Themes of Geography: *Location, Place, Region*

Objectives

Students will
1. design a color-key and boundary line map of Oceania's regions
2. define and evaluate prefix meanings for three Oceanic areas

Rationale

The Australia-New Zealand region is located south of the equator between the Pacific and Indian Oceans and southeast of Indonesia. The region is composed of the island continent Australia and the two islands of New Zealand. New Zealand is located 1,200 miles southeast of Australia.

The Melanesian region is located south of the equator, north of Australia, and extends east/northeast to encompass New Caledonia and the Fiji islands. New Guinea is the largest island in the region. Melanesians are dark-skinned.

Micronesia is north of the equator in the Pacific Ocean and is north of Melanesia. The islands in Micronesia are low islands. This is possibly the most difficult region to map with students. Large-scale maps that offer Oceania as a whole entity are not readily available. Therefore, it is important to spend sufficient time on mapping Oceania.

Skills Taught in This Unit

- Map reading
  - Relative location
  - Color and symbol keys
- Analysis
- Research

Vocabulary

Oceania *Polynesia* *Micronesia*
Melanesia *Trust Territories* *poly*
micro *melan/melano*

Regions Within Oceania

Although there are some minor conflicts about placement, the generally recognized regions in oceania are Australia-New Zealand and the Pacific region. The Pacific region is divided into the subregions of Micronesia, Melanesia, and Polynesia. (Notice, however, that New Zealand is included with Polynesia.)

Materials: world map or large-scale, Pacific-centered map; "Regions Within Oceania" activity sheet; pencils; outline, political map of Oceania (as large-scale as possible for students' use); colored pencils (or markers or crayons); rulers (or straightedge); dictionaries; reference books on Oceania

Directions
While displaying a world or Pacific-centered map, discuss with students the vastness of Oceania. Guide students' reading and mapping of the activity sheet. Discuss with them why prejudices can occur when identifying the Oceanic subregions.

Name ____________________

Regions Within Oceania

There are two major divisions in Oceania, Australia-New Zealand and the Pacific realm. Australia is the most well-known portion of *Oceania*. As the world's smallest continent, and a major continental island, Australia separates the Pacific and Indian Oceans. New Zealand is generally considered an overlapping nation that can be placed with either Australia or *Polynesia*. Many geographers place New Zealand with Australia instead of including it as the southern tip of Polynesia. Since the native Maoris of New Zealand are of Polynesian descent, it is easy to understand why New Zealand can also be included as part of Polynesia. The Pacific region includes Micronesia, Melanesia, and Polynesia. *Micronesia* is basically north of the equator and west of 180° longitude. *Melanesia* is mainly south of the equator and west of 180°. Polynesia is generally east of 180° longitude, both north and south of the equator.

Micronesia includes the Northern Mariana Islands, the Marshall Islands, Palau, the Federated States of Micronesia, Kiribati, Nauru, and the U.S. *Trust Territories* (Johnston Atoll, Wake, and Guam). Melanesia includes Papua New Guinea, the Solomon Islands, Vanuatu, Fiji, Wallis and Futuna Islands, and New Caledonia. Polynesia includes Midway Island, Hawaii, Tuvalu, Western Samoa, American Samoa, Cook Islands, Niue, Tokelau, Tonga, French Polynesia, Easter Island, Pitcairn Island, and New Zealand.

Using a globe and an atlas, do the following on a map of Oceania.

1. Color Australia yellow.
2. Draw lines to form the boundaries of Micronesia, Melanesia, and Polynesia and label each region by name.
3. Color New Zealand yellow, but also include it within the boundary of Polynesia.

Using a dictionary:

4. Define *micro*. ____________________
   Why does this describe Micronesia? ____________________
5. Define *melan* or *melano*. ____________________
   How does this apply to Melanesia? ____________________
6. Define *poly*. ____________________
   Why does this help define Polynesia? ____________________

Regions of Oceania

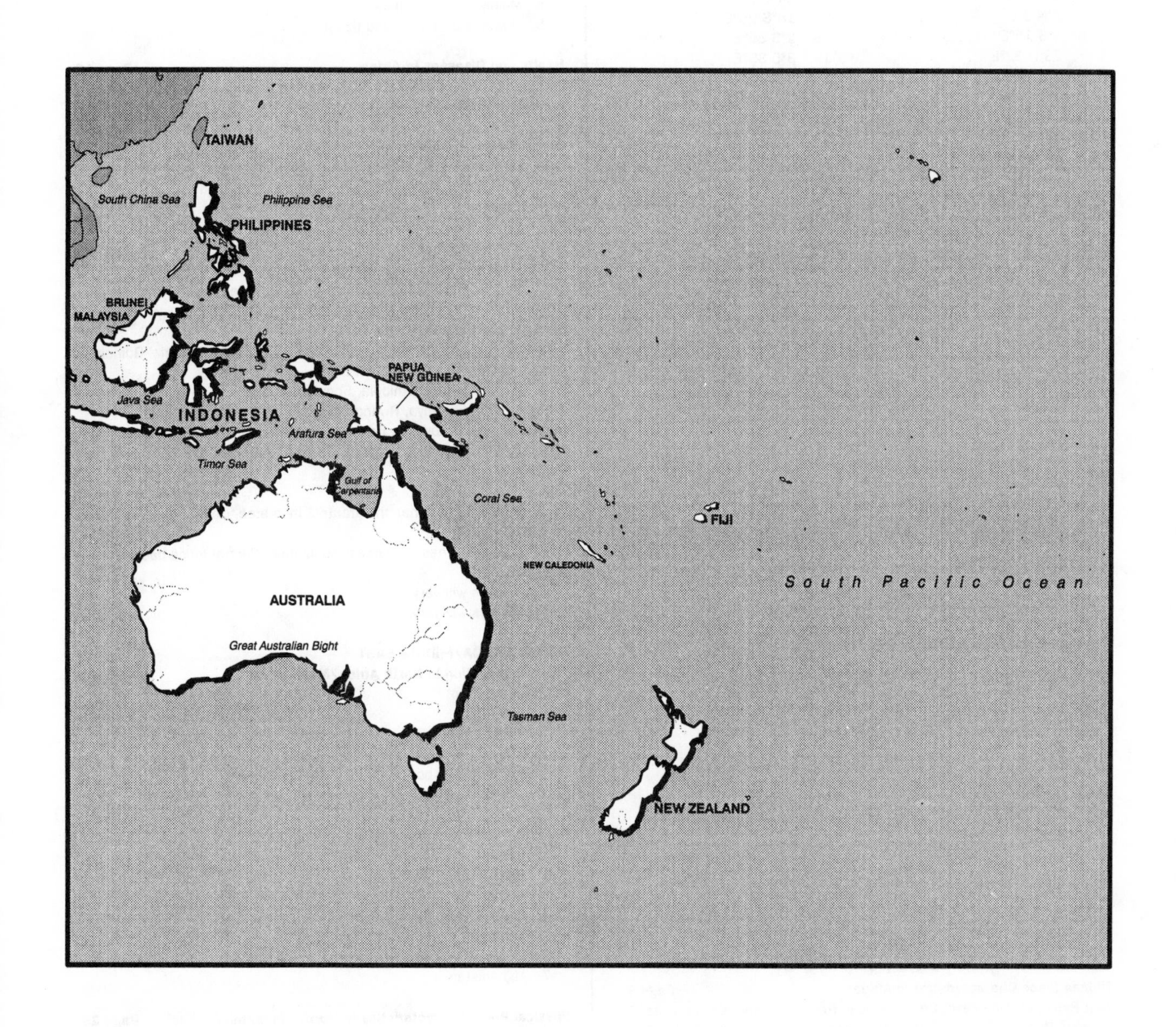

Answer Key

AFRICA

Absolute Location in Africa — Page 4

1. 3°S 37°E
2. 12°N 43°E
3. 16°N 33°E
4. 30°N 31°E
5. 7°N 3°E
6. 4°S 15°E
7. 23°N 32°E
8. 2°N 20°E
9. 12°N 4°E
10. 24°N 10°E
11. 23°S 22°E
12. 22°S 14°E
13. 1°S 33°E
14. 6°S 30°E
15. 34°S 19°E
16. 34°S 20°E
17. 18°S 25°E
18. 2°S 35°E
19. 3°S 35°E
20. 17°N 2°W
21. 23°S 14°E
22. 6°S 21°E
23. 34°S 21°E

Relative Location in Africa — Page 5

1. Most are located in the northern hemisphere, on the continent of Africa.
2. Egypt contains two. North Africa contains four.
3. The majority are in coastal locations.
4. Yes, six (Cairo, Kinshasa, Cape Town, Dakar, Addis Ababa, and Algiers) are their countries' national capitals.
5. Better opportunities, for jobs, housing, education are reasons why Africans choose to live here.

Physical Place Characteristics in Africa — Page 8

Human Place Characteristics in Africa — Page 9

red: Benin, Burkina Faso, Central African Republic, Chad, Congo, Cote d'Ivoire, Djibouti, Gabon, Guinea, Madagascar, Mali, Niger, Senegal, Togo, Zaire
blue: Botswana, Cameroon, Gambia, Ghana, Kenya, Liberia, Malawi, Mauritius, Namibia, Nigeria, Seychelles, Sierra Leone, Swaziland, Uganda, Zambia, Zimbabwe
orange: Angola, Cape Verde, Guinea-Bissau, Mozambique, Sao Tome & Principe
yellow: Equatorial Guinea
green: Algeria, Comoros, Egypt, Libya, Mauritania, Morocco, Sudan, Tunisia, Western Sahara
brown: Tanzania
uncolored: Burundi, Eritrea, Ethiopia, Lesotho, Rwanda, Somalia, South Africa

1. French (red) and English (blue) are the main languages, with some Arabic (green), Portuguese (orange), and Spanish (yellow), as well as indigenous languages (Somali-uncolored, Swahili-brown)
2. Mainly the western half of Africa
3. The eastern half of Africa, including southern Africa
4. Mainly northern Africa
5. Mostly with trading and travel

Health and Diseases in Africa — Page 12

The ten countries in Africa's AIDS region are Burundi, Congo, Kenya, Malawi, Rwanda, Tanzania, Uganda, Zaire, Zambia, and Zimbabwe.

Desertification in Africa — Page 13

Algeria, Senegal, Mali, Burkina Faso, Niger, Chad, Sudan, Eritrea, Djibouti, Ethiopia, Somalia, Kenya, and Madagascar are at high risk of becoming desert.

Regions Within Africa — Page 16

green: Algeria, Egypt, Libya, Morocco, Tunisia, Western Sahara
red: Benin, Burkina Faso, Cape Verde, Chad, Cote d'Ivoire, Gambia, Ghana, Guinea, Guinea-Bissau, Liberia, Mali, Mauritania, Niger, Nigeria, Senegal, Sierra Leone, Togo
yellow: Cameroon, Central African Republic, Congo, Equatorial Guinea, Gabon, Sao Tome and Principe, Zaire
blue: Djibouti, Eritrea, Ethiopia, Somalia, Sudan
orange: Burundi, Kenya, Rwanda, Seychelles, Tanzania, Uganda
purple: Angola, Botswana, Comoros, Lesotho, Madagascar, Malawi, Mauritius, Mozambique, Namibia, South Africa, Swaziland, Zambia, Zimbabwe

1. Southern Africa has the greatest land area. Central East Africa has the smallest.
2. West Africa has the largest population. Central Africa has the smallest.
3. Answers will vary.
4. Answers will vary.

NORTH AFRICA/MIDDLE EAST

Absolute Location in North Africa/Middle East — Page 21

Giza (Cairo), Egypt — 31°N 31°17'E
Alexandria, Egypt — 31°12'N 29°58'E

1. Iraq, Euphrates
2. Istanbul, Turkey, Marmara, Bosporus
3. Greece, Aegean
4. Turkey
5. Turkey
6. Mediterranean
7. Nile

Relative Location in North Africa/Middle East — Page 23

1. Turkey
2. Egypt
3. Israel
4. Saudi Arabia
5. Bahrain
6. Morocco
7. Afghanistan

Physical Place Characteristics in North Africa/Middle East — Page 26

1. An aquifer is an underground reservoir of water found in a porous, water-bearing rock layer of earth.
2. exotic
3. Egypt is the "gift of the Nile" found on the western side of the Fertile Crescent. Ancient Mesopotamia, present-day Iraq, was the "land between the two rivers" found on the eastern side of the Fertile Crescent. These river areas were known for their fertile soil and formed a crescent shape in the Middle East.
4. erg, hammada, reg, wadi, and oasis
5. *Sahara* means *desert* or *wilderness*.
   Rub-al-Khali means *Empty Quarter*.

Human Place Characteristics in North Africa/Middle East **Page 28**

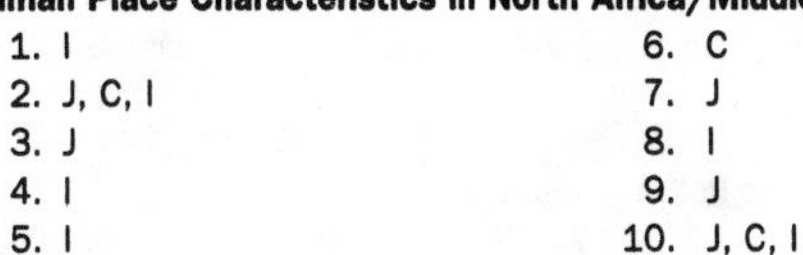

1. I
2. J, C, I
3. J
4. I
5. I
6. C
7. J
8. I
9. J
10. J, C, I

FREE: Afghanistan, Algeria, Bahrain, Cyprus, Egypt, Iraq, Israel, Jordan, Kuwait, Lebanon, Morocco, Oman, Qatar, Saudi Arabia, Syria, Tunisia, Turkey, United Arab Emirates, Yemen
NOT FREE: Iran, Libya

Oil and Water in North Africa/Middle East **Page 32**

1. 1869—Suez Canal opened
   1956—Suez-Sinai War; Suez Canal nationalized
   1960—OPEC created, five charter member nations
   1967—Six-Day War; Egypt sank ships and closed Suez Canal
   1973—Arab-Israeli War; oil embargo against Europe, Japan, and U.S.
   1979—OPEC produced 66% of world's oil
   1980—Iran-Iraq War; tripled oil prices
   1982—Oil prices plummeted
   1990—Persian Gulf War; Iraq invaded Kuwait
   1991—Iraq dumped oil into Persian Gulf
   1992—OPEC produced 41% of world's oil
3. Red; Suez Canal
4. 44.5%
5. 29,200 ships per year
6. 12.9 km./hour

Dams in North Africa/Middle East **Page 34**

1. Egypt
2. Turkey
3. Syria
4. Ataturk Dam
5. Aswan Dam
6. Aswan Dam
7. Turkey
8. Iraq
9. Syria
10. Egypt and Sudan
11. Turkey
12. Iraq
13. Egypt
14. Turkey

1. +
2. +
3. -
4. -
5. -
6. -
7. +
8. +

Regions Within North Africa/Middle East **Page 37**

green: Morocco, Algeria, Tunisia, (Western Sahara)
orange: Egypt
red: Iraq, Syria, Lebanon, Jordan, Israel
yellow: Turkey, Cyprus, Iran, Afghanistan
brown: Saudi Arabia, Yemen, Oman, the United Arab Emirates, Qatar, Bahrain, Kuwait

ASIA

Absolute Location in Asia **Page 42**

1. 8°S 111°E
2. 1°N 103°E
3. 5°N 114°E
4. 13°N 102°E
5. 23°N 90°E
6. 28°N 86°E
7. 18°N 72°E
8. 34°N 71°E
9. 29°N 33°E
10. 31°N 35°E
11. 41°N 29°E
12. 40°N 52°E
13. 81°N 40°E
14. 35°N 139°E
15. 37°N 127°E
16. 45°N 126°E
17. 39°N 116°E
18. 31°N 121°E
19. 21°N 115°E

Relative Location in Asia **Page 43**

1. Caspian Sea
2. South China Sea
3. Dead Sea
4. Arabian Peninsula
5. Lake Baikal
6. Bay of Bengal
7. Indonesia
8. Red Sea
9. Yellow River and Yellow Sea
10. Ob River

Physical Place Characteristics in Asia **Page 47**

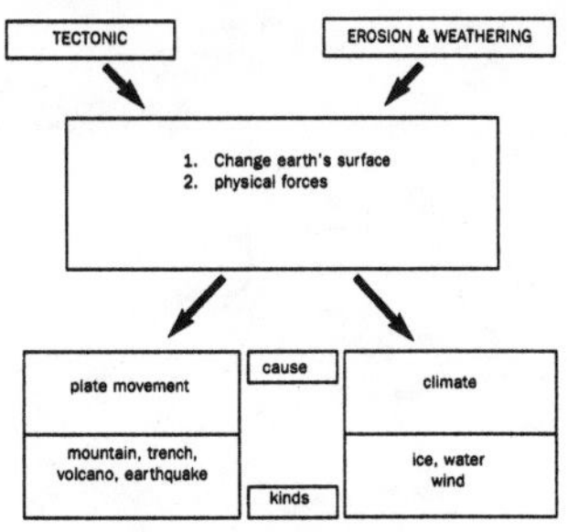

1. erosion and weathering
   tectonic
2. mountains and plateaus
3. trench
4. earthquake
5. climate
6. erosion
7. water; ice; wind

Human Place Characteristics in Asia **Page 49**

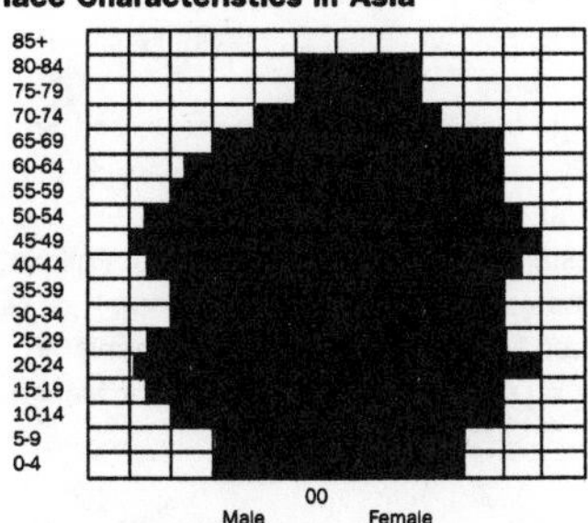

Page 50

1. Answers will vary.
2. Japan must convince its women of child-bearing age to have at least one child; government may have to redesign some jobs/occupations with less need for human labor and more use of technology/robots.
3. four per thousand
4. Japanese infants receive good prenatal care and good pediatric care; there are ample physicians and medical facilities to meet the demands and needs of Japan's children.
5. Japan's population pyramid should appear to have females living longer than males; females could outnumber males in some age groups.
6. The country's population will increase as citizens live longer.
7. People have better access to health care, possibly have better diets, and get enough exercise.
8. 75,600,105 people
9. big bulge
10. a. fewer babies
    b. lots and lots of workers
    c. lots of seniors
11. developing into being rich
12. under 15 years of age
13. Of these four Asian nations, Japan is growing at a slower rate than China, Indonesia, and India.
14. World War II with many adult Japanese males dying in battles, and the atomic bombing of Hiroshima and Nagasaki killing many Japanese
15. Asia's population will continue to increase; Japan's will be at a slower rate than some other Asian countries.

Technology in Asia **Page 53**

arithmetic, geometry, algebra, astronomy, writing systems, calendars, pyramids, arch, zero, decimal, plastic surgery, water clock, woven cotton, rust-proofed iron, paper, porcelain, seismograph, printed money, gunpowder, compass, abacus, silk and paper prints w/movable type and woodblock designs, mass-produced paper, video cassette, compact disc player

Agriculture in Asia **Page 55**

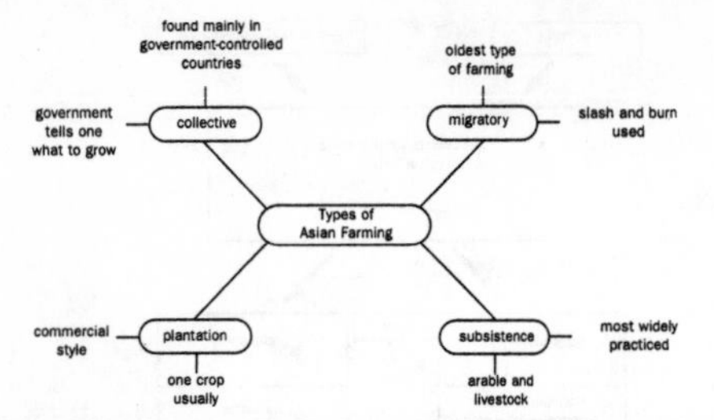

1. Fertile Crescent in Southwest Asia (Egypt's Nile River valley and Mesopotamia's Tigris and Euphrates river valley)
2. "Green Revolution"
3. rice and wheat
4. India, Japan, Malaysia, Pakistan, Philippines, Taiwan, and Turkey
5. Indigenous trees are cut down, topsoil is burned as trees/stumps are also burned, destroying nutrients in topsoil; reforestation is often not practiced.

Regions Within Asia **Page 58**

purple: Russia
green: Afghanistan, Armenia, Azerbaijan, Bahrain, Cyprus, Georgia, Iran, Iraq, Israel, Jordan, Kuwait, Lebanon, Oman, Qatar, Saudi Arabia, Syria, the United Arab Emirates, and Yemen; diagonal possibilities: Sinai Peninsula (Egypt), Anatolia Peninsula (Turkey)
blue: Bangladesh, Bhutan, India, Maldives, Nepal, Pakistan, and Sri Lanka
yellow: China, Japan, North Korea, South Korea, and Taiwan; diagonal possibilities: Hong Kong, Macau
red: Brunei, Myanmar, Indonesia, Cambodia, Laos, Malaysia, Philippines, Singapore, Thailand, and Vietnam; diagonal possibility: Papua New Guinea
orange: Kazakhstan, Kyrgyzstan, Mongolia, Tajikistan, Turkmenistan, Uzbekistan, and Russia (Siberia); diagonal possibilities: Inner Mongolia, Zinjiang-Uygur, and Tibet

EUROPE

Absolute Location in Europe **Page 63**

1. 51° N 0°
2. 41° N 12° E
3. 60° N 24° E
4. 55° N 37° E
5. 51° N 51° E
6. Answers will vary.
7. 11:00 P.M.
8. 2:00 P.M.
9. 64° N 21° E
10. 38° N 9° W
11. 3° N 6° W
12. 40° N 3° W
13. 5:00 A.M.
14. 6:00 A.M.
15. the same, Wednesday
16. nothing, it is still the same
17. Thursday
18. traveling west across seven time zones and not crossing the International Date Line
19. traveling west crossing the International Date Line, add a day
20. in a great-circle route over the Arctic Ocean
21. Answers will vary.
    Possibilities: to be able to conduct international business and to estimate times
22. Answers will vary.
    Possibilities: to be able to conserve aviation fuel, which is quite expensive, to be able to take the shortest amount of time when traveling

Relative Location in Europe **Page 65**

1. Scandinavian; North
2. Jutland; Baltic
3. Mediterranean; Pyrenees; Iberian
4. Italian; Mediterranean; Tyrrhenian
5. Italy; Rome
6. Balkan; Ionian; Aegean
7. southern; Crete
8. Hungary
   Switzerland
   Moldova
   Macedonia
9. Spain; Mediterranean
10. British; Scotland
11. Northern Ireland; Irish
12. Ural; Europe; Caspian; Black

Possible causes: cold and warm ocean currents, winds, mountains
Possible effects: winds bring rain, mild, wet winters, sunny dry summers, flora and fauna

Human Place Characteristics in Europe **Page 70**

1. Scandinavia
2. Southern
3. Southern
4. British Isles
5. Central
6. France and Low Countries
7. Southern
8. Eastern
9. Southern
10. Southern
11. Eastern
12. France and Low Countries
13. Scandinavia
14. Southern
15. Southern
16. British Isles
17. Central
18. Eastern
19. Scandinavia
20. Southern
21. British Isles
22. France and Low Countries
23. Central
24. France and Low Countries
25. Southern
26. Eastern
27. Southern
28. Eastern
29. Southern
30. Eastern
31. Eastern
32. Eastern

Movement of Trade in Europe **Page 74**

1. all 15 nations
2. Hungary; Iceland; Malta; Norway; Poland; Romania; Russia; Switzerland; Yugoslavia
3. Answers will vary. Possible answer: Germany is centrally located, already established as a major industrial nation, German currency (mark) well-recognized as a world currency
4. Portugal
5. Answers will vary. Possible answer: Luxembourg is a neighboring nation of Belgium, they have a customs union with Belgium, both nations use the franc as their currency, and Belgium is quite dependent on its foreign trade.
6. Answers will vary. Possible answer: Norway already trades heavily with EU nations, and was scheduled to join EU in 1995, but Nov. 1994 referendum voted this down.

Air Pollution in Europe **Page 76**

1. W
2. S
3. W
4. W
5. O
6. O
7. O
8. W
9. T
10. S
11. O
12. T
13. T
14. S
15. O
16. T
17. N
18. O
19. W

Regions Within Europe **Page 79**

purple: Norway, Sweden, Finland, Estonia, Denmark, British Isles, Iceland, and Greenland
red: the Netherlands, Belgium, and France
orange: Germany, Switzerland, and Austria
blue: Russia, Latvia, Lithuania, Belarus, Poland, Ukraine, Slovakia, Czech Republic, Hungary, Romania, Moldova, Bulgaria, Macedonia, Albania, Montenegro, Bosnia and Herzegovina, Croatia, Slovenia, Serbia, western parts of Kazakhstan, Georgia, Azerbaijan, and Turkey
yellow: Greece, Italy, Malta, Spain, Portugal, Crete, Sicily, Sardinia, and Corsica

NORTH AMERICA

Absolute Location in North America **Page 85**

1. Answers will vary.
2. Tallahassee
3. "N" stands for north, "W" for west; "N" could be from the Northern Hemisphere, "W" from the Western Hemisphere
4. T6N; R20W
5. Florida
6. FL
7. Pensacola—904
8. 11 A.M.